Riitta Lahtinen, Russ Palmer
& Merja Lahtinen

Environmental Description

for visually and dual sensory impaired people

Environmental Description
for visually and dual sensory impaired people

Copyright:
© 2010 Riitta Lahtinen, Russ Palmer & Merja Lahtinen
First published in Finnish 2009

Published by:
A1 Management UK

All rights reserved. No part of this publication may be reproduced or transmitted in any material form or by any means, electronic or mechanical including photocopying, recording or by an information storage or retrieval system, without the written permission from the authors and publisher except as may be permitted by the Copyright Act or in the case of brief quotation embodied in critical articles or reviews.

A Cataloguing in Publication record for this book is available from The British Library.

Cover design, interior text layout and illustrations:
Ari Palo (www.aripalo.fi)

Photographs:
Kalle Kiviniemi, Merja Lahtinen, Virve Lindholm, Anita Palo, Tanja Ristimäki

Printed by:
Art-Print Oy, Helsinki/Finland, 2010

ISBN 978-0-9550323-2-5

Foreword - towards description

The aim of Environmental description is to support the use of description in everyday situations with visually and dual sensory impaired people.

Environmental description defines thoughts on description; what it is and which are the principles when describing information. In this book description is related to a deeper analysis of the target and furthermore various methods of description are presented. Description supports actions and choices of a person with visual and dual sensory impairment and facilitates contacts with the environment. Description supplements experiences perceived through various senses and it widens the possibilities for participation of persons with visual impairment.

The book gives ideas, guidelines and tools for a basis of environmental description. Examples and ideas of various factors, situations, preparations and wishes that influence description have been collected. In addition, the book includes exercises on various areas of description. Environmental description has been written both from the describer's and the receiver's point of view. The book can be recommended for instance to people of any age with visual impairment, dual sensory impairment and acquired deafblindness, as well as to someone with communication disorder, family members and carers, friends and professionals. It provides a basic educational study book for professionals wishing to supplement their knowledge of how to apply different techniques in description, including audio description for museums and art exhibitions.

The text includes comments and experiences of description in authentic situations from people with dual sensory impairment. Often our actions and participation are somehow based on receiving and processing visual information. If you cannot see or hear, environmental description is one way to share information. Description will also provide experiences. It is based on the receiver's interest in the subject and the describer's competence to describe accordingly. This book will encourage the describer and the receiver to reflect together what they wish to share by means of environmental description. The receiver can guide the describer from his/her own standpoint, and they can agree on description methods at the beginning of the situation. Good instructions help the describer to make an environmental description to that matches the receiver's needs.

This book was written by three authors. Riitta Lahtinen and Russ Palmer have been testing and using environmental description in their everyday life for 20 years. Riitta has trained various professional groups in environmental description since 1995, such as teachers, sign language interpreters, instructors, deafblind and visual impaired people, as well as people close to them. She is one of the teachers in the educational programme of audio description for describers for visually impaired and has been analyzing various areas, methods and fundamentals of environmental description. Riitta's special focus area of interest and research is how to use the body in environmental description connected to social-haptic communication. Haptices and haptemes are explained further in her doctoral dissertation (Lahtinen, 2008a). In this book Russ will tell about his own experiences on environmental description and analyze them as a receiver with dual sensory impairment. Russ and Riitta have been developing environmental description together.

The third author is Merja Lahtinen, who has been working as a special class teacher for 20 years. As a teacher for children and youth with verbal and perception disorders and visual impairment she has practical experience of how a conscious use of environmental description can help students perceive the environment and various situations, use independent initiative and participate – this supports learning!

Acknowledgements

We would like to thank following people who commented on the text and provided examples related to description: Anne Paavolainen, special needs assistant for visually impaired students; Tanja Ristimäki, sign language interpreter and Riikka Hokkanen, physiotherapist for children with visual impairment.

Thank you Anita Palo and Tanja Ristimäki for letting us use your photos. Thanks to Kalle Kiviniemi, The Finnish Deafblind Association, for photographing and giving technical support. Many thanks to Leena Zacho for the English translation, Jane Haynes and Stina Ojala for the proofreading, Julie Usher and Anthony Stamp for their comments and Ari Palo for his art design and graphics.

And many thanks to all of you, who for the last 15 years have participated in education on environmental description and given valuable comments on the availability of description. Special thanks to Pirkko Pölönen and Anita Palo who, as receivers of environmental description, have shared their thoughts with us about how a clear description should be produced and about the many possibilities of description.

This book is published in Finland with the support of Friends of the Blind, The Support Foundation for Blind Children, and The Finnish Association of Non-Fiction Writers, The Association of Mobility and Low Vision Instructors and The Finnish Deafblind Association. Special thanks to The Service Foundation for the Deaf and the director Hilkka Nousiainen.

Special thanks to Aili and Matias Lahtinen, and Peter and Colleen Palmer for their love and support.

Helsinki – Frinton on Sea – Jyväskylä 01.02.2010

Riitta Lahtinen
MEd, PhD.
Mobility and low vision instructor,
Sign language interpreter,
Audio describer

Russ Palmer
Music Therapist SRAT(M)

Merja Lahtinen
MEd, Special teacher of the visually impaired

ENVIRONMENTAL DESCRIPTION
for visually and dual sensory impaired people

Foreword - towards description 3
Acknowledgements 5

CONTENTS

Tables, figures and pictures 8
Thoughts for the reader 9

1 Definition of description 10
   1.1 What is description? 12
   1.2 Sensory perceptions as basis of description 18

2 Characteristics of environmental description 22
   2.1 Neutral and subjective description 24
   2.2 Factors that influence description 30
   2.3 Clear and functional description 37
   2.4 Auxiliary devices used during description 39

3 Classification of description 42
   3.1 Description according to languages and methods 42
   3.2 Description according to interaction and methods 44
   3.3 From wide description into details 48

4 Description to various receivers 55
   4.1 Description given to children and young people with
       visual impairment 55
   4.2 Audio description as service for people with visual impairment 61
   4.3 Description in everyday life of people with dual sensory
       impairment and deafblindness 63
   4.4 Describing the auditory world to a person with hearing
       impairment 69

5 Description in different situations ... 71
- 5.1 Description of people and their behaviour ... 71
- 5.2 Description of new internal space ... 75
- 5.3 Describing landscape, architecture and buildings ... 81
- 5.4 Description of a hotel room and accommodation ... 84
- 5.5 Description of menu and buffet ... 86
- 5.6 Description of arts ... 89
  - 5.6.1 Description of an individual work of art ... 91
  - 5.6.2 Description of a photo ... 94
  - 5.6.3 Description of theatre and music performances ... 97
  - 5.6.4 Description of films ... 97

6 Description of colours, details and special situations ... 100
- 6.1 Description of colours ... 100
  - 6.1.1 Basic colours experienced by people with visual impairment ... 102
  - 6.1.2 The meaning of colours ... 104
- 6.2 Describing appearances ... 106
- 6.3 Description of advertisements ... 109
- 6.4 Description of different situations ... 112

7 Describing onto the body ... 120
- 7.1 Use of hands and objects during description ... 121
- 7.2 Body and movements during description ... 123
- 7.3 Drawing onto the body ... 127
- 7.4 Describing hobbies onto the body ... 129

8 Pointing directions ... 134

References ... 142

Supplementary material ... 144

TABLES, FIGURES AND PICTURES

Table 1. Characteristics of individual and group description 31

Figure 1. Description according to languages and methods 43
Figure 2. Interaction and methods of description 44
Figure 3. From wide description into details 49
Figure 4. Map of a meeting room 79
Figure 5. Facts about the artwork 91
Figure 6. Different sizes of pictures 107
Figure 7. Basic maps of bowling and adapted Curling drawn onto the back 130
Figure 8. Description of music and dance onto the body 132
Figure 9. A clock face with a person in the middle 137
Figure 10. Examples of a plate and a table as clock faces 137
Figure 11. Points of a compass 139

Picture 1. Book cover 25
Picture 2. Using a torch while exploring the dashboard of an airplane 39
Picture 3. Exploring a miniature of the Colosseum 40
Picture 4. Mökä in a sweater 56
Picture 5. Showing applause onto a body 65
Picture 6. Emotional response hand and different parts of the body 74
Picture 7. The Hall 78
Picture 8. Old Frinton by the Sea 90
Picture 9. Statue 92
Picture 10. Mökä having an ice-cream 93
Picture 11. Frans Leijon and a woman on a tandem 95
Picture 12. Group photo 96
Picture 13. "A candle in the church" bobbin lace 117
Picture 14. Describing the flight paths of airplanes 131
Picture 15. A clock face on a person's back 138
Picture 16. Finding a star in the night sky 140

Thoughts for the reader

"Maybe one of the most difficult things for a sighted person to appreciate is how much of the visual environmental information a dual sensory impaired person misses out. That is why even description that seems of minor importance in everyday life can make a big difference for the quality of life in a family, with friends and colleagues. In Finland and Scandinavia environmental description is part of the education and training of sign language interpreters. Description allows both visual and dual sensory impaired people to have information of better quality in a spontaneous manner.

In this book Riitta, Merja and I have incorporated experiences from personal, family and professional points of view. It has been a great challenge to write this book, as well as a rewarding experience. During the writing process I have become even more consciously aware about how much information it is possible to share by touch through social-haptic communication.

I hope that the reader will get an insight and is able to experience how the environmental information can be shared – sometimes by using very simple, yet effective methods. Part of them we already use naturally, but we may not always be aware of them.

I can tell from my personal experience, that environmental description has enriched my life in a way I could not imagine was possible to experience as an almost blind person using a cochlear implant and a hearing aid. Environmental description gives me an equal access to information. Various areas of life, such as experiencing arts and hobbies, can be supported by means of environmental description. In addition to safety information, it also includes descriptions of amusing and funny situations."

Russ Palmer

1 Definition of description

Descriptions can be heard daily in many everyday situations used by various professional groups. By descriptions they give clues to actions, tell about the order of activities, anticipate upcoming situations, and describe what the target looks like. For instance, reporting and commenting things can be heard on the radio, seen on the TV, read in the newspapers and advertisements, they are included in train announcements, promoting products, and discussions between doctors and patients. There is description in hobbies, such as in instructions how to set up a model train or how to crochet. In clothes and textiles there are care labels telling about the material and size. By means of description you can answer questions about what something looks like, sounds like or what action is produced.

For example...

- *"Parrot plea*
- *Our African Grey parrot went missing from its cage in the garden on May 4 about 2.15 pm. His name is George. He looks ugly, is going bald on his breast and he has red feathers on his tail. He is not used to flying and walks like a little old man. He will talk and whistle at you but he is not very good when he is handled. If you have seen him, please phone..."*
- - Lost and Found Pets -section

- *"We'll now make a U-turn."*
-   – Taxi driver

- *"The restaurant car is located in coach number four from the back of this train. Helsinki station is on the left hand side when facing the front of the train."*
-   - Train conductor

- *"Now I'll press harder to establish contact with the next tooth..."*
- – Dentist

- *"This is bus number 62."*
-   – Bus driver to a person with visual impairment standing at the bus stop

- *"On the front face of this coin there is the profile of emperor Troy. On the reverse side of the coin there are pictures of various gods."*
- – Telephone salesman about a Roman coin

- *"There is room for six bottles in the long side of the crate and for four on the short side. You can have 24 bottles in the crate in all."*
-   – TV advert

- *"Where is Jean? Jean Birch, a 25-year-old from London, disappeared on Tuesday, 2nd January. She is approximately 5 ft 5 tall with fair hair and strong body. At the time of her disappearance she was wearing jeans, a yellow winter coat, a long, black, knitted scarf and was carrying a blue back bag. She was last seen..."*
- - Missing Persons announcement

- *"You are allowed to carry one piece of hand luggage (56 x 45 x 25 cm)."*
-   - Information leaflets at the airport

1.1 What is description?

With the help of conscious environmental description you can share information on visual and auditory environment or specific targets. Environmental description makes things and activities in the environment clearer, which enables easier access to contexts; it aims to give a holistic view of the target, so that the receiver would master it better by being aware of what is happening around them. Environmental description complements a person's sensory perceptions; it supports visual sensations about what has been seen and provides information for the support of tactile sensation. In addition, environmental description facilitates the person by enabling contacts with targets in the environment and within social situations. It will be easier for a person to orientate in his/her surrounding space, when he/she receives information on the environment, surrounding space, objects and their placement, people and their reactions as well as the atmosphere. Information received by environmental description can be used as a basis for action.

When you master the environmental basic issues, your independence, awareness and possibilities to choose actions increase. The feeling of security will increase at the same time with the awareness of special or surprising environmental obstacles. (Smith, 1994) Description will make it possible to get independent access to information, since the person in question will also explore objects and get acquainted with the space either by himself/herself or together with a partner through the partner's guiding hand. Environmental description can be thought to be a description of general, physical, personal and social space and action, where visual (sight), auditory (hearing) and other sensory information is shared with the receiver either spoken (written) or sign language, vocally (creating sound effects), producing sounds (instruments) or in another agreed form (pointing, touch, drawing, movement etc.) (Lahtinen, 2004; Lahtinen & Palmer, 1996; 1997; Raanes, 2004).

Anything visual can be selected from the environment to be described, for instance people (behaviour, action), objects, natural elements (plant, animal, scenery), spaces (indoors, outdoors), vehicles, arts (painting, picture, statue), materials, colours and forms as well as other auditory information (music, rhythm). Environmental description is needed especially in changing situations. Changes, threats, level differences (steps, slope) and surprising actions are told so that the person can be prepared for them. The receiver of a description gives information on whether the description should be continued or not, and what in the target interests him/her. This is done by giving feedback and reactions to description. Previous experiences of the described target help the person to understand and create a holistic picture of the target even if the describer had not succeeded in conveying everything. Sometimes the describer's and the receiver's mental images differ from each another, and misunderstandings may occur. Then you have to describe again, discuss it and maybe use other concepts and make the description more profound.

According to people who are born blind, description gives a wider visual picture of the world. In accordance with them, you can speak to people with visual impairment issues related to sight, such as colours and the beauty or ugliness of a target (Honkanen & Vartio, 1998). People with dual sensory impairment or acquired deafblindness said that the description of targets is part of the interpreting process. Basic issues that had to be described according to the 32 interviewees were as follows: environment in general, surroundings, people and everything connected to the interactive situation so that it was possible to act accordingly in a spontaneous way. They wanted to know if there was anything special in the environment, activities, changing situations, what the others were doing, landscapes and colours. In addition, they wanted to know if there were changes in the environment compared with the initial situation; if people changed seats, if someone left the meeting or if pieces of furniture were moved. They also wanted information about funny and amusing situations, changes in the emotional atmosphere and entering of catering. (Lahtinen, 2004)

Authors with visual impairment have in various articles expressed their experiences and need for description. For instance, one has to have courage to describe and interpret for a visually impaired person, but on the other hand not by giving everything on the plate, but by giving the visually impaired person the joy of making their own conclusion (Tiihonen, 2004). There are many situations in everyday life, where environmental description helps. Various methods of description can be used such as use of the body.

Voipio (2007, 12) writes as follows:

> "At one time we realized with my family, that it was possible to illustrate many things to me by drawing. Of course it is more pleasant to explore embosses, but you need proper emboss tools and time for using them. I don't mean maps and other graphs that are for long-term use, but like temporary, off-hand situations that need an explanation.
>
> The back of a blind person is a good drawing board. The broader the back, the wider picture you can draw. When an issue or phenomenon must be illustrated, it can be done by drawing on the back. Of course you can describe some things onto the palm or arm as well, but the illustrations there tend to become rather limited.
>
> If the conversation around the coffee table turns to the profile of Sydney Opera House or a Swiss pine, I can soon figure it out if someone draws with their finger the outlines on my back. Or when we are walking and pass an interesting entrance gate I can get an idea of its structure, when it is outlined onto the surface of my jacket. I also draw describing pictures on the backs of my sighted friends - and at the end wipe the drawings carefully away.
>
> I have often got lost when walking alone on some route, since while walking slowly I have not been able to realize, where the routes turn to. If I mention this to someone, he/she can draw the map on my back. It is as if the curves and turns settle down by themselves on a mental map. Next time I come to the same place I just use that map, and won't get lost anymore."

Receiving description can be a lengthy process if the methods are not applied correctly. It is demanding using residual hearing and sight in noisy and dark surroundings, or maybe the person does not have the experience on how to gain more control of the situation through description. The idea of guidelines for describing is that the receiver can express how he/she wants to receive description in various situations. Functional and fluent methods and changes in them also give variation and different sensations. In environmental description context is of special importance, for instance if the premises or exhibition are new, if you are buying clothes or listening to a competition. Especially people with dual sensory impairment or acquired deafblindness need to use various methods by which they can receive more quality information and get a better control of their environment.

Printed texts, adverts, literature etc. include basic description aimed at everyone. Environmental description especially helps those with low vision, blindness, hearing impairment, dual sensory impairment, elderly people, people with perceptual disorders and everyone who needs support in receiving visual information. (Lahtinen, Lahtinen & Paavolainen, 2006) Both auditory and visual impressions are described for people with dual sensory impairment and acquired deafblindness, which makes the person feel involved, since he/she has knowledge of general things about the environment. When a person has functional vision, the possible perception of visual information will be taken into account. When description is produced by signing in free space, you must ensure it is received. In that case, for instance suitable signing distance, illumination and place are clarified. Distance to the target of description may vary: it can be looked at from short and/or long distance. For a person with hearing impairment even the description of sound environment is included.

Anyone can be a describer; a family member or various professional groups for instance teachers, assistants, nurses, sign language interpreters, audio describers, mobility instructors and art producers. Description is connected with services provided by various professional groups. For instance during guiding many blind and visually impaired people are interested in hearing descriptions of the environment and landscape. Guiding situation does not usually prerequisite other than necessary description, for instance factors causing insecurity and weird sound sources are described. (Törrönen & Onnela, 1999) Moving together may be a more pleasant experience, when the perception of environment is shared. (Lahtinen et.al. 2006) For instance while walking in the city, visual impaired persons can ask sighted people to describe public buildings, statues and display windows (Honkanen & Vartio, 1998).

For visually impaired people description is connected to different situations and often includes reading the text on the target. The following is a summary of descriptive targets in the course of one week:

- describing during joint action
  (TV programmes, train and airplane tickets)
- describing of things brought into, taken from and placed in the personal space
- describing space and landscape during guiding
  (while walking, in a car, in public vehicles)
- describing during dining situations; description of menu, what is on the table and portion
- describing a buffet
- describing routes and maps
  (distance, placement, stable/changing information)
- describing people
  (those present, appearance, clothing, people approaching/leaving)
- describing objects (forms, colours, naming sources of sound)
- describing new products
- describing a room layout and objects
- describing a person's own clothes (colours, models, materials)
- describing the location of where to write a signature
- describing hobbies and arts
  (theatre, paintings, pictures, photos, movies, DVD)
- describing movements during exercises
- describing newspapers, papers, letters, Christmas cards, advertisements, forms and presents
- describing objects inside a box and cupboards
- describing non-verbal information and silent moments

Pictures are explained by words, so that pictures, graphs and pieces of art in a book are translated into verbal and/or written explanations. A picture explanation can be combined with feeling embossed pictures. A picture explanation makes it easier to perceive a complicated emboss or graph material. In a picture explanation information on the picture is compared with familiar things and objects, for instance size with the size of an egg or one's own body. A picture explanation tells what the picture is comprised of; you do not interpret or make conclusions. The aim is to express the information in the picture clearly, objectively and with a language accessible to the receiver. (Eeronen, 2002; Hietaketo-Vieno, Kartovaara, Mäntylä, Pyötsiä & Salo, 2000; Lahtinen et. al. 2006) The explanation includes what the picture is about and what is special about it (Honkanen & Vartio, 1998).

Description is closely connected with a commentary which can be heard by anyone. Sports commentaries are general descriptions of activities and happenings in a situation. Reporting is quick, intensive and often bound to real-time, such as a description of a hundred metre race. Manuscripts, travel reports and diagrams are written commentaries.

1.2 Sensory perceptions as basis of description

A person describing the environment to another is actively observing the environment and using all their senses in order to collect the data. The describer will transfer visual information to a person with visual impairment, so that "a visual story will be translated into words" (Honkanen & Vartio, 1998, 151). In addition to information received by vision and hearing, the describer can use sensory information received through other senses, such as touch (change in temperature, draft from a window/door) and vibrations from various surfaces (music through the floor), smell (bakery, cafeteria, leather shop, candle) and taste (lettuce). Apart from visual and other senses we even experience the visual world through mental processes. According to Sava (2007) this is connected to both thinking and imagining. Perception is an interactive relationship between a perceiver and a target, continuing in time and space actively and selective.

According to Jakes (2003), the concept of environment is wide, multiple and connected with various situations that are transformable, variable and overlapping. The environment can be divided into a natural or man-made environment. The natural environment can be an original environment, which human beings have not touched. The man-made environment can be divided into materials (houses, towns, roads) and objects, created environments such as human relations (friendship, marriage, family), mental and cultural things (language, science, art, law, policy, ethics, religion).

The describer has to verbalize information transmitted by eye and sight, i.e. he/she has to encode it to a row of concepts. When you verbally tell the others about what you have seen in the environment, you change the three dimensional picture to a one dimensional word flow. Information received by one gaze takes several minutes when expressed verbally. Describing a target with sign language is fluent since elements connected to visual modality, such as places, relations and the speed of motion are parts of the language. Even if the receiver could not sign, he/she can enjoy art through the hand movements. In order to make transmitting information quicker, you can support verbal information by using body and touch at the same time.

The describer must be visually literate. That means understanding of visual order of the object world, physical environment and illustrated targets. In order to develop one's visual literacy, the person must understand some facts of seeing. The person has to be able to produce descriptions to another and communicate them, i.e. command how to verbalize visual experiences. People often learn basics of visual literacy quite naturally. A smiling person is usually understood to manifest happiness. The visual reality in the environment consists of an established order, regularity and cultural meaning are included in that (traffic signs). The visual order of the environment is often related to the functions of objects in everyday activities. It is natural, that the coffee packet is near the coffee machine. Certain constantly repeated routes become a mental map, which helps in planning actions. (Seppänen, 2002) Environmental description cannot offer everything from the visual world, but it is possible to receive part of that experience.

What you look at is what you see of the target. Seeing is often connected with the spectator's relation to the target. Is description one way of accessing the picture? Heikkonen (2005, 1) writes in the editorial of Airut, Finnish magazine for visually impaired, about "Hated, loved picture":

- *"...The picture is for instance without text or without an informative text about what it really illustrates. Sometimes the frustration is triggered by the use of various verbally inaccessible tables and diagrams, from which the sighted participants immediately have perceived the core of information in question.*

- *One interesting feature is connected with looking at pictures by people with visual impairment. If you get only a picture you most often cannot tell, what it illustrates. But if someone tells you, what the picture represents, you kind of begin seeing - you know, what you should find in the picture. That is why the purpose of picture captions for perceiving the pictures is in that sense essential. For a blind person picture captions are often the only way to receive information about pictures.*

- *Sometimes for a person with low vision pictures are even easier to perceive holistically than a live target. A friend of mine who has severe*

> *tunnel vision said once, that she always sees only one eye or ear of people, but on a photo in a newspaper she has seen, how those people really look like as a whole. Here a whole is more than the sum of its parts.*
>
> *Ultimately, some kind of a golden mean might be best when it comes to pictures. We cannot exclude pictures from our world; they are part of the majority culture and provide information even to those with visual impairment, although not exactly in the same way as to sighted people. We should rather speak about the accessibility of pictures rather than resist them..."*

We also get information about the environment haptically. Haptic information is transmitted by skin, hands, arms, feet, legs and the whole body. According to Gibson (1966) it is possible to observe haptically the geometric characteristics (form, dimension, gradient etc.), surface features (structure, roughness, smoothness), materials (mass, hardness etc.) and relative temperature. With blind children the exploring with hands is connected with development of certain levels. The characteristics of an object can be felt by hands as well as its temperature, consistence, size and weight. Gradually they develop the concepts related to form and start comparing the elements. Differentiating forms, arcs and contours is connected with perceiving graphic information.

Exercises and reflections

The concept of description
1. What is environmental description?

Various descriptions
2. Collect different environmental descriptions from magazines.

3. Which professionals provide environmental description?

4. Listen to radio programmes and read literature; they include descriptions of people, actions and locations.

Exploring objects
5. Explore different objects with your eyes closed. What information do you receive about the objects by touch?

2 Characteristics of environmental description

There are many things that influence environmental description. Environmental description can be divided into at least four areas. These are: expression of basic characteristics, basic description, precise description and extended description. Basic characteristics include a short explanation of the properties of the target (an advertising leaflet). Basic description means the target and action are described for the receiver's needs by explaining basic aspects about the target. Precise description includes description of details of the target to give the receiver an overall view of that. In addition to precise description, extended description includes background information on the target, such as personal history of an artist, genre or other relevant information.

Depending on time available, description can be short and concise or longer and more detailed. A short description may be just a concise answer to a question. For instance to a question if the blouse is transparent, the answer can be a short "yes". When a person asks where his white cane is, the answer could be "under your chair, on the right hand side". The person may ask if a blouse is blue, and a possible answer could be "yes, it is dark blue". In a more detailed description you explain more precisely, e.g.:

- *"The blouse is dark blue. It is dark blue velvet with light blue wavy lines*
- *shining slightly through. The wavy lines are vertical. In a certain light the*
- *blouse looks dark blue, whereas in another light the lighter wavy lines*
- *stand out more. From a distance the blouse looks dark blue."*

In this situation, the description is precise, spontaneous, responding to the interest created in the situation and the receiver's motivated search for information. When it comes to description of large premises, such as a department store, you first describe the information counter and information on the map by naming general lines for moving in the destination (names of stores, departments). More detailed description will be carried out at the different departments.

The describer may prepare the description beforehand or it may be spontaneous i.e. produced at the time. When moving together the description is often spontaneous. When travelling, shopping or visiting new places the describer does not necessarily know beforehand what comes next. When entering a train the receiver may suggest: "Tell me if you notice something special or interesting while we are walking". The describer can beforehand visit the exhibition or do internet-based research. Description can also be given afterwards, such as describing the musicians during the interval at a concert. In some cases it is not possible to describe during the concert without causing a disturbance.

A systematic way of description can be trained. The description of a target can be started outwards from oneself or from the outside towards oneself, from inside out or from outside in, from up to down or down to up, from front to back or back to front, left to right or right to left. Many people with visual impairment would rather have descriptions outwards from themselves, since they are making a map of the place in their mind at the same time. When the describer has chosen the description direction, many visually impaired people prefer the description to proceed logically. The description begins to advance from the place, where the two people are standing. There the person with visual impairment can feel where he/she is standing and sense his/her own location. Description connects a person to their environment, in cases where the receiver cannot do this relying on his/her own senses only. Describing premises and landscapes outwards from oneself is clear. From down to up description works well when describing for instance growing (trees) or moving directions (flames from a fire). Description of an ice-cream cone can be from down to up describing ("First we scoop the chocolate ball, then the vanilla and finally the strawberry."). When a person has an ice-cream cone in his/her hand, the description can be from up to down ("First there is a strawberry ball, then the vanilla and finally chocolate.").

2.1 Neutral and subjective description

The describer interprets the target he/she is describing. Earlier experiences, knowledge, strategies, culture, competence on a subject or on plenitude of matters have an influence on how he/she will choose to describe the target. Some targets include several meanings (adverts). Visual and/or auditory art have an effect on people in general and thus even on the describer. During a description some verbal or linguistic emphasizing may occur. The describer may try to forward information and emotions to the listener by varying rhythm, dynamic and tone of the voice. Some of the receivers mention, that describers should not bring their own thoughts and conclusions into their description, whereas others wish, that describers also share their personal interpretations and experiences.

Various descriptions of the same target
Same target can be described in many different ways. The output of each describer is slightly different. If the describer has wider and more detailed expertise on a subject, the description may become more precise. However, the describer does not always have this knowledge, which makes him/her describe using general concepts. The following example is a description of the same flowerbed first in general concepts and then more precisely:

- *- There are red, blue, yellow and pink flowers in the flowerbed.*
-
- *- There are red pelargoniums, blue primulas, yellow petunias and*
- *pink lilies in the flowerbed.*

The describer's presentation will consist of the items she chooses from the target, word choices, and the order in which she will present them. In the following example three different people describe the same book cover (picture 1) to different target groups.

Picture 1. Book cover

Person 1. The aim of the description is to serve as a precise literal presentation for a reader:

- *"Book text and lay-out of two hands are placed on a purple background. The shade of purple varies from dark to light purple. In the middle of the book there are two hands, his and hers. The hands are visible from the elbows, palms down. They are reaching towards each other, one on the top of the other forming a horizontal line. Her hand and lower arm are above his lower arm. Some black shirt sleeve can be seen on the top of his arm. Her hand, fingers and thumb are touching his arm. The touch is light. Her red nails are clear. Otherwise the picture is slightly out of focus and stylish, shadows have been added.*

- *Under the hand contact there is a black text "Riitta M. Lahtinen, PhD". Above the hands there is the text "Haptices and Haptemes". Words "Haptices and" stand on one line and under them there is the word "Haptemes". In the word "Haptices", there is an arrow pointing up on the letter H's left arm and on its right arm there is an arrow pointing down. They form arrows pointing up and down connected by the horizontal part of letter H. Above the picture there is the text "A Case study of developmental process in social-haptic communication of acquired deafblind people."*

Person 2. The receiver of this description is a senior pupil. Description is closely connected with showing by hands. Then the describer shows with the help of the receiver's hands, how the hands are placed on the cover of the book:

- *"This is a book cover. The cover page has been divided into three areas. On the top there is the name of the book. Under that there is a specification of the name and in the middle there is a picture. The general colouring of the picture is purple. The light purple on the top gets darker towards the bottom.*

- *At the bottom of the book there is the name of the author, "Riitta M. Lahtinen, PhD", written in black letters. On the top of the book there is the name of the book "Haptices and Haptemes", also in black, but written in bigger letters than the name of the author. On the first arm of letter H in "Haptices", there is an arrow pointing up, and on the other arm there is an arrow pointing down. Arrows are also used in the text pages of the book in order to show the direction of movement.*

- *In the middle of the cover there is a picture of two hands. The right hand of a person reaching from the right side almost to the left side has been illustrated from the elbow to fingers. On the right side you can see a darker shirt sleeve. The hand is in a peaceful position palm down, the thumb is slightly apart from the other fingers. The other hand comes from the left and is stretched above the before mentioned hand. This is the left hand of a person, palm down and on the arm of the first-mentioned hand. The left hand thumb is slightly apart from the rest of the fingers and the nails are painted red.*

- *Above the hands there is a text "A Case study of developmental process in social-haptic communication of acquired deafblind people". The text is written in black and smaller print than the title the book and name of the author."*

Person 3. This description is concise; it is part of a bigger unity in an event (Ristimäki, 2008):

- *"On the projector screen there is the front page of Riitta Lahtinen's dissertation. On the top of the cover there is a text "Haptices and Haptemes". Under the text there is a picture of two hands. The fingernails are painted red on the left-side hand. Both hands are palm down. Stretched fingers of the other hand touch the other person's arm. Above the picture there is the following text: "A Case study of developmental process in social-haptic communication of acquired deafblind people."*

In a neutral description the describer aims at consciously choosing things from the target without relating her personal sensations to those and by being as neutral as possible. From a neutral description the receiver can make his own interpretation. You can choose certain issues from arts, of which everyone can share experiences (basic form, line, direction, design), but even the experience of colours can differ subjectively. On the other hand, someone can see in the picture of hands the hands of an aged granny whereas someone else can see hands of a hard working person, when the same image is interpreted in different ways. It demands courage from the describer to change a visual view into words. The describer must dare to say, if the target for instance looks strange (Tiihonen, 2004). The describer forwards what he/she sees whether it is positive or not.

With subjective concepts you can highlight the atmosphere of a target, an essential idea, which will not open up by a neutral description only. Description of an everyday target which is related to action is easier when done neutrally. Then again, in the arts the target can be visual, changing by vision in the spectator's mind to a subjective and aesthetic experience. It is challenging to transform this into a neutral description. Sometimes a description is experienced neutral, even though there are comparisons (amount, ratio) inside the expression:

- *- She is 5 ft 5 in height and he is 5 ft 10. She is shorter.*

The difference between neutral and subjective description will appear in different alternative descriptions of Helene Schjerfbeck´s painting "The Convalescent". The first example aims at neutral description and the second includes subjective parts of description.

Neutral description:

> "In the front of the painting there is a wicker chair on the left where a 7-year-old girl is sitting wrapped in a sheet. On the right there is a dark wooden table. The hands of the girl are reaching for a china mug on the table which contains a branch with opening buds bending towards her hand. The background of the painting is filled with a book shelf, where only the lowest shelves are visible. There are big books on the shelves. Books can be distinguished as books, even though more precise details are not visible.
>
> The colours of the painting are various shades of brown, black, white and green. The light brown wicker chair becomes even brighter due to sun shining through the window. The sun light is partly passing through the twines of the chair. The white colour is emphasized by a big pillow on the chair partly covering the back rest. The girl is wearing a black long sleeve dress onto which a long sheet has been wrapped. The sheet covers her body from her armpits down. The dark wooden table is partly shining in the sun. The feet of the table are round.
>
> She is frail. She is looking at the branch in her hand. Her uncombed hair is brown and short. The blue eyed girl has slightly red cheeks. The wicker chair is a big arm chair, the back rest of which is high and curved. She reaches half way up the back rest. There is a separate softened chair pad, which can be distinguished under her and the sheet.
>
> On the table under her hands there is a white china cup. Its only decoration is a blue figure spot. Her one hand is holding the cup and with the other hand she is holding the branch between her fingers. The branch is bent towards her face and window. On the top and stem of the branch there are some greenish, opening leaves. On the table around the cup there

- *are dry leaves. On the opposite side of the table there is a glass ink well*
- *on paper. On the furthermost side of the table there are two paperback*
- *books one on the other. Behind the books there is a red flower, looking*
- *like a carnation."*

Subjective description:

- *"A young girl has been carried from her sick bed into a wicker chair in the*
- *library. Since the room is cool, she has been wrapped in a white sheet.*
- *She is already better and able to show some interest in her environment.*
- *There are no objects of her own on the table. She is interested in a branch*
- *in a mug. The branch has been taken from a berry bush in the garden. It is*
- *still winter outside and they are waiting for spring. Flowers have not yet*
- *risen onto the surface of the earth. She is sitting straight upright on the*
- *chair. She is waiting for something...maybe for her room to be cleaned."*

On Ateneum's website you will find examples of extended description, which include even background information on artists and additional explanations. Collecting background information on a piece of art, artist, personal history and era is usually done by the employees of the scene of art (Välttilä, 2008). An example of this is an extended description of the background of "The Convalescent", which can be found on the following website (www.edu.fi/oppimateriaalit/kultakausi/heletoip).

2.2 Factors that influence description

Description can be carried out physically on the spot (close description) or far away from the target (distant description). You can for instance describe an image sent by computer or mobile phone, by describing it physically at a different location and the description will be transmitted by audio or text formats or using a webcam (sign language). Description can be carried out (Lahtinen et.al. 2006):

- spontaneously and in real time,
- in joint action by describing the events systematically,
- as a beforehand prepared description (pre-prepared description),
- beforehand recorded or written description and
- as consecutive description (post-poned description) after the event if some issues, reasons or consequences remain unclear.

When a target to be described is hard to put into words because of its ambiguity, it can be compared to another similar object or target: "There is a lamp made of thin, light paper like an angular wasp nest hanging from the ceiling.". Syntax or choice of vocabulary may reveal an ambiguity of the target or show difficulty to choose precise describing words. The following underlined examples show expressions related to ambiguity or interpretation:

- The flower vase is <u>rather</u> delicate and roundish.
- The flowers are <u>possibly</u> roses.
- There are <u>obviously</u> sweets in the glass bowl.
- She is wearing a <u>reddish</u> blouse.
- This path is <u>remarkably</u> narrower than the previous one.
- There are cherry tomatoes on the plate, <u>presumably</u> marinated.
- She <u>looks like</u> a model.
- There are <u>about</u> a dozen people in the living room.
- The surface of the table <u>seems a bit</u> worn.
- <u>You get an impression</u> that the movie scene is on a high hill.
- Two gable roofs create a <u>castle-like</u> atmosphere in the building.

The person's own experience and background will always be present when he/she is receiving description. Description may refer to a previous joint experience ("Right in front of us there is the so called pulley, which you exercised upper back muscles with last time you came to the gym."). Description can be identified through an everyday experience ("This hill is almost the same height as if you took the stairs to the fourth floor.").

The target group of a description may be one person (individual, personal description) or a group (group description). The size of the group may vary from two to many dozens (theatre). In principle there is no limit to the size of the group, since the description may be, for instance, a recording. Listening to a ready-made audio description with headphones is neither dependent on the describer's nor the receiver's timetable as used in some museums. Describing to one person is slightly different than describing to a group regarding options. Differences in these characteristics are shown in table 1.

Table 1. Characteristics of individual and group description

Characteristic	Individual description	Group description
audibility of the voice	close description, receiver's individual auditory devices	use of microphone and loop system
methods of description	receiver's wishes of description methods, changes of methods during description e.g. describing and drawing while moving easier to carry out	mostly general methods of description, limited changes in methods
reciprocal description	functions	functions
use of audio description	functions	functions
use of raised images	functions	one for each person or circulate to others?
pointing at directions in description, use of clock system	functions	with a group you have to agree how to express directions
touch and haptic exploration	functions	time and place must be arranged
use of guiding hand	functions	functions, if a personal guide is present (mirroring)
place	even smaller space is enough	a group needs more space

In the planning of a describing event you should pay attention to things that can influence description and perceiving processes such as:

1. Personal history of the receiver

Contents of description are based on the receiver's wishes and needs. Situations may vary from one day to another according to physical state, visual status, interest and motivation or orientation ability. Some people need more information. In individual description the activity level of the receiver and how much feedback the person needs for supporting his actions, may influence the amount and extent of information included in the description. For instance, when a person is ill or at the doctor's, he/she will only be able to receive functionally relevant descriptive facts.

A person listening through a loop system receives information given exclusively by the speaker. Sometimes the description can be spoken quietly into a hearing aid, for instance in M/T position or into a microphone during a theatre play. Description may be given in sign language a part of which consists of locating places and objects. When using sign language you should check if hands-on signing (tactile signing) or signing in free space is the most appropriate. If there are people with visual impairment in the audience who receive signing in free space, you have to pay attention to the pace and extent of signing etc. The fact that receiving is demanding becomes clear, when you describe to a person with deafblindness, since tactile signing can be physically demanding. In describing it is important that the speaker or signer keeps an unhurried tempo. During description the receivers use their imagination and a suitable pace gives them time to create mental images.

Before describing you go through the description instructions and agree on terms i.e. if the describer may use different methods, such as drawing onto body and if the target may be demonstrated with objects. Sitting at a table in a coffee bar you can describe relations and buildings with salt and pepper pots or sugar cubes. Lego bricks can be used to build targets or you can choose to design forms of a target with Play-Doh. You can use your own clothes and everyday objects to support the description. A scarf can represent the movement of a lake, the white cane can show the length or the form of the target can be teared out of paper. You can ask beforehand, if raised images of the targets already exist. The receiver's wishes regarding the methods of description will guide the describer to choose the best description option.

While planning a description you can think how much the receiver's different senses will participate in experiencing the description. In addition to the use of hearing and vision, a target can be related to with the use of smell and taste as well as haptics. An optimal functional use of vision is taken into consideration in description events by using beneficial lighting. Some people need good quality general lighting, while others prefer dim lighting because of it is not dazzling. It is often easier to perceive the described target, if there is sufficient good quality general lighting and a spot light on the objects. If the lighting levels of the premises change, you must take into account the adaptation of the visually impaired person's eyes regarding the new light. There must not be any disturbing movement, window or other source of light behind the describer and the pointed objects because of potential dazzling.

When the describer and receiver have joint experiences and memories of the target, those can be used during the description, which makes the perception faster. People can recall memories for many years. Regarding the choice of words; attention is paid for instance to the concepts and vocabulary of the receiver commands, since the general knowledge of elements in the environment, buildings or nature may vary from one person to another. The use of concepts describing pieces of art is demanding for both the describer and receiver, if they have no special interest or studies of the described target, for instance modern art. Even if the describer had the command of concepts of a special field, the receiver might not know them. In that case the concepts are also given everyday names, for instance about perspective in a painting:

- *There is a road in the bottom of the picture painted as a broad lane disappears into a pine forest on the upper right hand side. The wagon road is getting narrower, so that when it reaches the forest, it is only a narrow line.*

2. Issues related to event and place

In anticipation of a description events can be related in advance (The Finnish Independence Day Reception; description and evaluation of dresses). At exhibitions and museums individual objects are chosen to be described, whereas in various hobbies you can choose actions and results. In social events (party) you describe people present, how many, clothes, discussions and actions.

In description you take into account the relevance of the place and character of actions, for instance if the same place is used repeatedly or just once, which is the person's relation to the place (social or work place) and what is most important for the flow of actions (security, emergency exits). The possibility for describing a place can be influenced by others present. At the doctor's appointment the doctor may ask how you are when he opens the door, which gives no opportunity for description at that time. A fast description of the room, naming those who are present and special issues may sometimes be important in order to master the situation and secure one's integrity.

People have different methods of perceiving things, places and distances as well as making a mental map. Descriptions become more concrete if the person with visual impairment can at the same time move and explore the environment. Routes between targets are chosen so that there are no obstacles in the way.

A miscellaneous description and disorganized flow of information may cause a chaotic picture of a situation. If the description jumps between various targets at the same time, it is hard to perceive them. When visual information is received verbally, it is easier to perceive the targets when they have been clearly classified and rhythmitized to separate modules of description. Of course you can make comparisons between the targets.

3. The describer's choice

Anybody can act as describer, an educated person working in this area or an employee at a certain place telling about the target. In addition to contents, the describer must pay attention to his/her use of voice. In big premises the voice has to be loud enough and in some situations silent, even whispering.

When describing outdoors, you have to pay attention to the clothes you are wearing as well (rain, frost).

4. Description mode
Modes of description vary depending on the target and/or audience. The describer can be a general describer of an event (in a conference into a microphone), when the receivers cannot actually influence the mode of description. In smaller groups the description can be carried out as a dialogue, where the receivers may ask questions.

5. Time reserved for description
You must reserve enough time for describing, if you intend to explore and experiment with objects in a situation. Simultaneous presenting and getting acquainted with different targets in a hurry will not work, which is why it is good to separate these actions. It is recommended you arrive in good time, so that you have time before the event to get acquainted with the location and the activities, for instance at a theatre the actors´ voices, costumes and stage decor. Separating actions is related to the description planning, such as presenting targets, independent exploration and giving further information. First you name the objects and relevant contexts (Tupperware presentation: exploring is connected with a more precise description).

6. Ethics and proximity
The target is described despite its positive or negative contents. Sometimes an embarrassed and unsure touch onto the body may feel uncomfortable, whereas a functional, natural and secure grasp adds information to the description.

7. Informing about description
The describer can beforehand inform about an event that will be described in magazines for the visually impaired by sending personal messages or hand-outs. An example of a hand-out sent beforehand via the internet by a describer (Ristimäki, 2008):

- *"My name is Tanja Ristimäki. I am studying to become a sign language interpreter and will be a describer for the dissertation. Before the dissertation I will describe the auditorium. In the beginning of the public defence of doctoral thesis I will describe the doctoral candidate, custodian and opponent, and at the end of the event their departure. The microphones in the front of the hall are sensitive. The acoustics in the hall, such as echoing sounds as well as air conditioning in the hall may disturb the loop system. We kindly ask the audience to keep silent during the event in order for the loop system to work optimally. We also ask you to keep your mobile phones switched off."*

2.3 Clear and functional description

It is easier to plan and carry out a clear and functional description, when you know the client and his/her interests. In that case you are also familiar with the function of the receiver's senses, as well as the concepts you can use.

Clear description
- supports the receiver's participation,
- benefits from the receiver's earlier experiences,
- is relevant, meaningful and uses methods that have been agreed on together,
- supports the receiver's hearing and/or sight,
- advances logically and forms a logical entity,
- keeps the style constant,
- advances from general to detailed,
- advances from naming the context into exploring the object and more precise description,
- is rhythmitized according to how the things proceed, for instance listening, showing and experimenting are broken into sequences suitable for the listener,
- pays attention to things that can be of interest or meaningful to the receiver (helps in orientation and movements on location),
- includes the correction of wrongly perceived things and
- fits the time frames.

At an exhibition the objects can be described in the same order that they are displayed. Sometimes there is plenty of information present at the time and the describer must decide how he/she will proceed: which information to describe first: the name of the artist and the method by which the piece is made, or rather to describe the work itself first? The order depends on what the listener prefers. Some people prefer to create themselves a mental picture first and not only after they receive the name of the artwork. The instruction "proceed from big to small" does not always work. If the person for instance has a narrow vision field, he can first visually search for an area of the target, so that a figure can be built and perceived by different parts. For instance, the describing of Marimekko's poppy pattern on a tea mug can begin from the middle of the pattern:

- *- The core of the flower is black. It is surrounded by a yellow circle around which there are five red petals. The stem of the flower is black.*

Exploration of an object related to description can be done before or after the description. Sometimes it is best to explore independently before giving a general description, when the receiver's perceptions are supported by description. You can receive valuable information on an object independently, for instance about size, material, weight and moving parts. (e.g. Lahtinen et.al. 2006; Raanes, 2004) When it is possible for the person to touch and explore an object the description will include guiding the person's hand to the explored object. Sometimes description and guiding are closely related, for instance during personal description.

Descriptive expressions of stable and perceivable land marks are connected with locating the target and place. When the action is repeated (repeated use of the same route), the recognizable and named land marks orientates the route and space and allows independent movements. Light from windows and light spots, clearly distinguishable contrasts and/or guide markings give information for perceiving the direction and orientation.

2.4 Auxiliary devices used during description

During description it is possible to use various technical aids for seeing, hearing and exploring. The describer may have a pointer (ruler, pencil) or a miniature illustrating the target or raised image. Raised images are made e.g. of subjects taught at school such as maps, plants and animals. Also various art institutions, such as museums, make paintings accessible as raised images. They are explored through image reading i.e. exploring with hands.

If it is not possible to explore every subject with one's hands, you can demonstrate it with materials (fabric, metal, stone), smell and taste (spice, fruit) or source of sound (music, original speech). The describer may amplify the sound with a microphone. For exploring objects there might be cotton or vinyl gloves available near the exhibition. You can ask for them at the reception of an art exhibition, museum etc. At the same time you can inquire whether there are any recordings, raised pictures or Braille on the subject. After exploration you can use hand wipes (dusty, sticky targets).

People may carry their own technical aids, such as various eye glasses for indoor and outdoor use (reading, dazzling). There can be a presentation book, exhibition catalogue and images about the target available, where you can show the target to be described. A magnifier is used for reading the text about the target and in order to see details. Binoculars facilitate perceiving details further away. A torch is practical when looking at a dark target and when giving directions, as at an air museum enlightening an airplane dashboard (picture 2).

Picture 2. Using a torch while exploring the dashboard of an airplane

A guide dog and white cane assist moving. Various hearing aids and a personal microphone facilitate speech perception. Along with a person with visual impairment may be a guide, personal assistant or sign language interpreter.

It is good to get acquainted with a possible miniature in advance. It may help in perceiving the target, such as a big and wide architectonic construction (picture 3). When exploring a miniature you usually need a plain table. Some people may carry paper and a thick black felt-tipped pen that produces text, which is easily distinguishable on paper. In some locations you can find visual aids, such as a magnifying TV.

Picture 3. Exploring a miniature of the Colosseum

Exercises and reflections

Issues influencing description
1. What influences description?

Various descriptions
2. How does the description of the cover of the book in chapter 2.1 by three people differ from each other (use of time, details of description, target group)?

3. How does description for one person or for a group differ from each other?

Preparations for description
4. You are going to the Science Museum in London to describe the Moon Landing exhibition. How do you prepare for that?

Neutral and subjective description
5. How do neutral and subjective descriptions differ from each other?

6. Underline in the following text the neutral objective concepts with blue and subjective concepts with red.

At the hotel pool
It is an early morning. The sky is blue and cloudless anticipating a hot day. Only a couple of people have gathered to the hotel pool. The water in the pool is turquoise, clear and clean. Two people are swimming in the pool. One of them has grey hair, he is an elderly skinny gentleman and the other one is a sporty young woman. She is wearing a streamlined swimsuit, which occasionally flashes onto the surface while she is swimming fast from one end of the pool to the other. There are plastic lounge chairs by the pool. There are about 30 of them. A 50-year-old woman is sitting on one of them reading this morning's newspaper on her lap. She is wearing a small bikini and she has an even tan. On the table beside her there is a large mug full of green tea and a can of expensive sun lotion.

3 Classification of description

3.1 Description according to languages and methods

Description is divided into different areas according to language and method. In addition to verbal description (spoken, written or sign language) it can be produced with various sounds. Othman (1987) built sound images into paintings, with which she captured the atmosphere. Her work "Kuunneltuja kuvia" (Listened images) consists of a text read aloud, sound effects (sounds of crackling fire place, pulling a heavy bucket, axe chopping tree, footsteps in snow) and raised images. The images are made by an embossing method and the art has been simplified in order to make them clearer. An example of a sound scenery is background sounds related to Helen Schjerfbeck's "The Convalescent"; a bird singing, music, a pendulum's movement inside a long case clock, heavy breathing, the distant murmur of talk, the rustling of a wicker chair and the faint rattling of furniture.

Stories told with the help of human voice and vocalization without words, have also been defined as "pieces of sound" (Röholm, 2008). In voice description you can use either your own voice or other sources of sound, for instance musical instruments, animal sounds, objects (shoes) or body parts (hands, feet). An example of a presentation with voice description could be a pantomime song or playing the piano with your voice (aaaAAAaaa, tom-Tom-Tom-tom) (Lahtinen, 2008b).

Using the body as a part of description (drawing, describing with movement and objects) is further discussed in chapter 7, whereas chapter 1.2 focuses on exploring the target from a haptic approach. You may find miniatures or objects of the targets to be described. There may already be photos or raised images of that particular object. By means of developing technology, such as GPS, navigator program and talking mobile phone, we have various ways to facilitate the mastering of the environment as in orientation, positioning, distances, finding the target or routes. (Tenhami, 2008) These support the provision of basic information on location and orientation. Description according to languages and methods has been collected in figure 1.

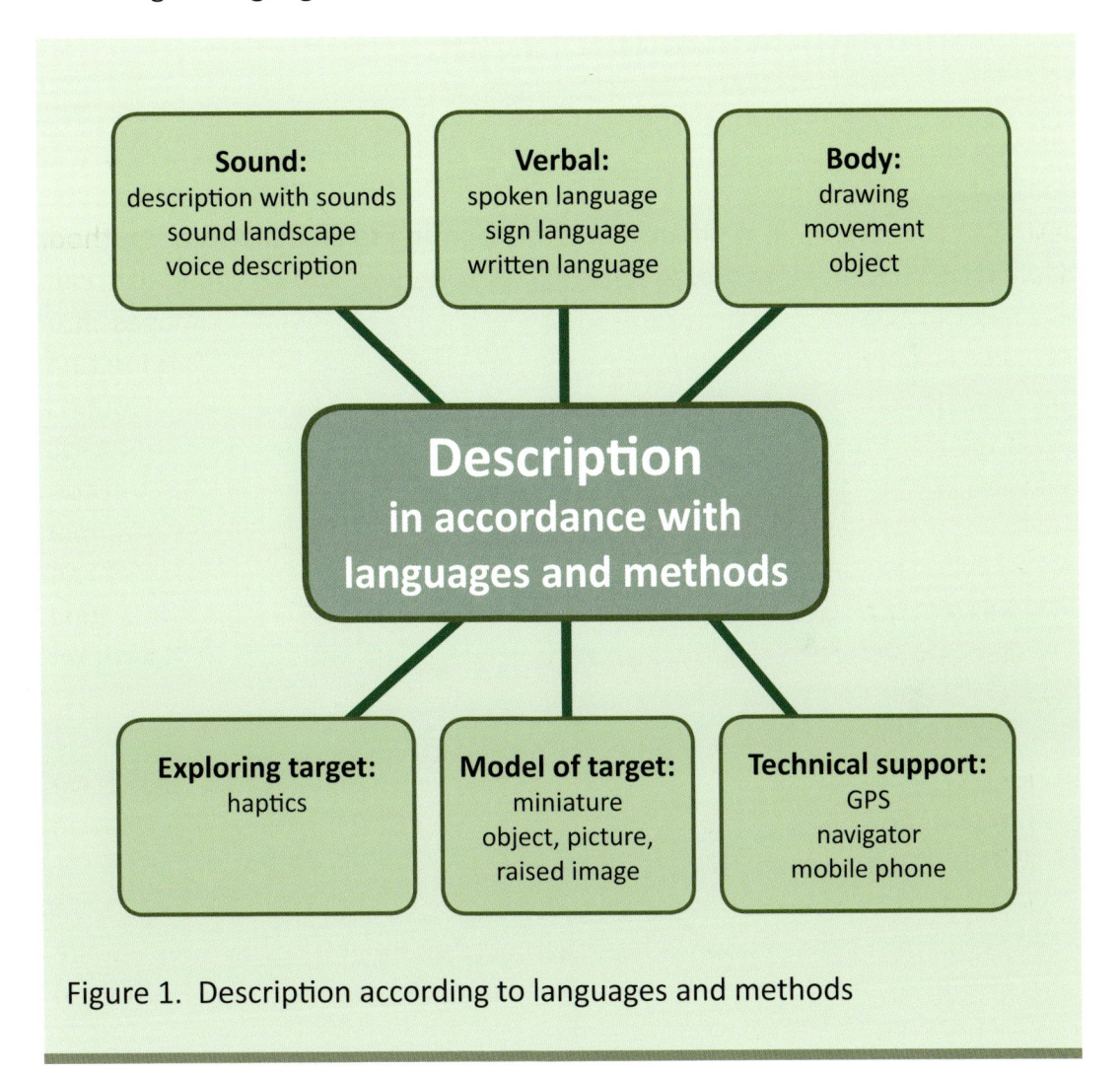

Sound:
description with sounds
sound landscape
voice description

Verbal:
spoken language
sign language
written language

Body:
drawing
movement
object

Description in accordance with languages and methods

Exploring target:
haptics

Model of target:
miniature object, picture, raised image

Technical support:
GPS
navigator
mobile phone

Figure 1. Description according to languages and methods

3.2 Description according to interaction and methods

Description can also be classified by situational interaction and methods. The description situation between the describer and receiver may be a one-way description or a dialogue i.e. the listener can be a mere receiver or actively asking and commenting. Considering these factors, description situations have been divided into eight areas, figure 2 (e.g. Lahtinen, 2001a; 2004; Lahtinen et al., 2006).

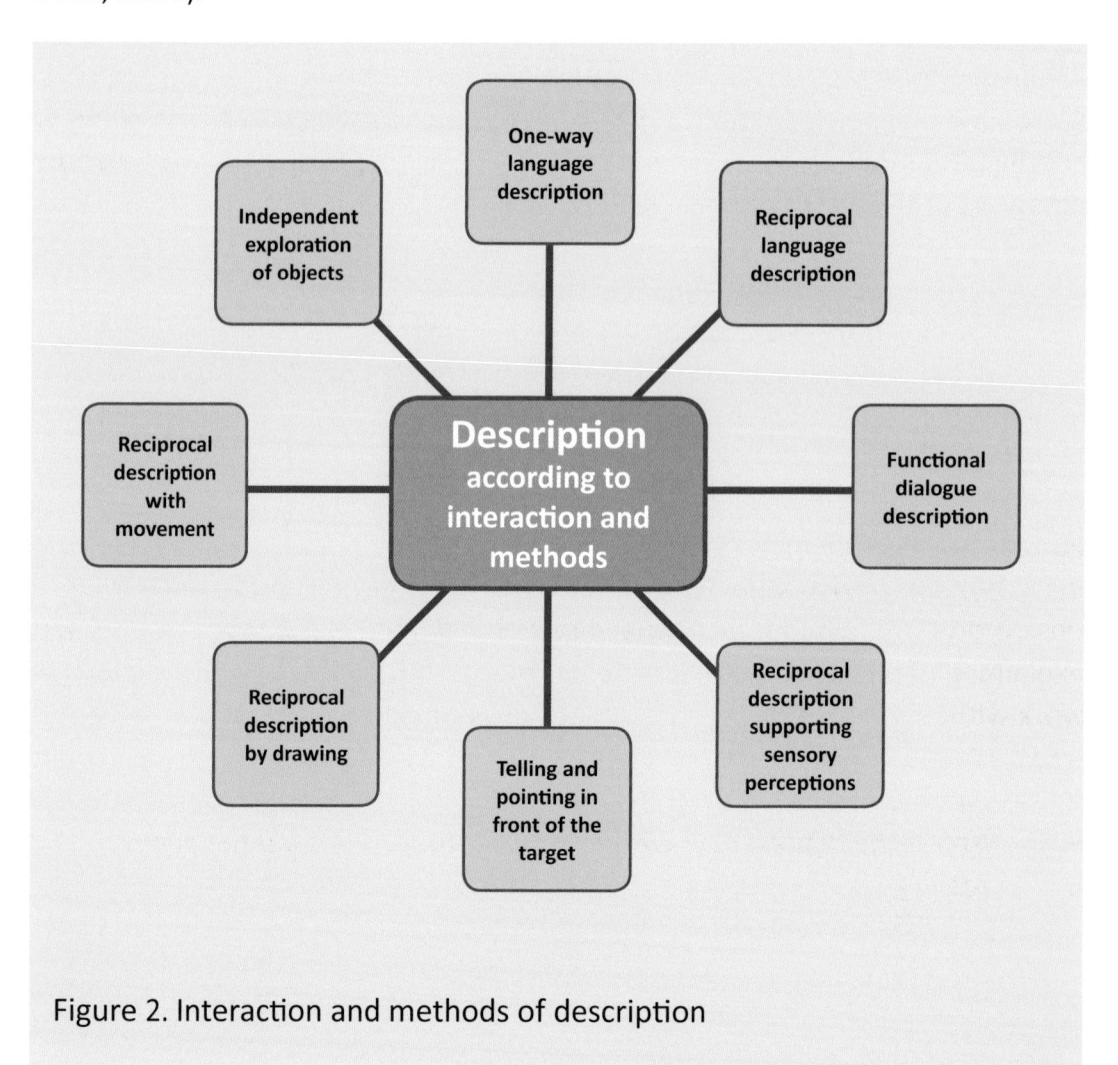

Figure 2. Interaction and methods of description

- One-way language description
- Reciprocal language description
- Functional dialogue description
- Reciprocal description supporting sensory perceptions
- Telling and pointing in front of the target
- Reciprocal description by drawing
- Reciprocal description with movement
- Independent exploration of objects

One-way language description

Description works with spoken language, sign language, recordings or written language. During a one-way description the receiver cannot comment or ask questions. An example of this is describing the assembly hall for the pupils at a spring party:

- - *There is a big spring birch on the left hand side of the stage. It has small light green leaves. Upstage there are five smaller birches. The hall is decorated with flowers, wood anemones and pennyworts made by pupils.*

Reciprocal language description i.e. dialogue description

During a dialogue description the receiver asks questions, gives comments or specifications. For instance, in winter when walking on the pavement a snow plough approaches:

- - *A snow plough is coming towards us.*
- - *What is a snow plough?*
- - *A snow plough is a semicircle plate placed diagonally in front of a car. When the plough is down; snow will fly to the side of the pavement.*

Functional dialogue description

In a functional dialogue description the receiver will add touch-related description to the target using the guiding hand, for instance euro coins when explaining of new money. The describer may also have an object to explore or work with, e.g. some clay or other material connected with crafts.

- - *Pick a 50 cent coin from the money.*
- - *Isn't it the biggest coin with deep indentations around the edge?*
- - *Yes.*

Reciprocal description supporting sensory perceptions
Description may be given to different sources of smell as in various basins of a sewage treatment plant, or by telling that the loud and surprising noise came from the dustcart when it reversed into the yard. In the following example two people are slowing down as they approach the traffic lights on a tandem bicycle:

- - Why are we slowing down?
- - We are coming to the traffic lights. They are red, you can hear the
-   beeping sound.

Telling and pointing in front of the target
Pointing can be carried out simultaneously, alternating or sequentially during description. Different hand forms and movements are used within the guiding hand in addition to pointing in front of the target. Pointing can be used for instance to show how the lecturer's talk is proceeding on the receiver's paper with a finger, pencil, ruler etc.

Reciprocal description by drawing
Drawing onto the body can clarify the forms and relations to the target to support description. Forms and directions can be drawn onto the receiver's hand, palm, back, various surfaces (table, wall) or in the air in front of the target. In studying different school subjects, such as in a history class, the maps are drawn onto the pupil's back or hand. The route of a bowling ball in gym class can be described onto the pupil's back.

Reciprocal description with movement
Description with movement can be carried out by using the describer's own body (role, position, rhythm), which allows the receiver to explore through the describer's body how the target is expressed, or the receiver can make the movement with his/her own body. For instance when exploring a statue, either the describer's or receiver's body will be used. The target may also be made together using both bodies, when they are both moving simultaneously or they each have their own "roles" (movement, position). In physical education the movements and functions that are needed will be shown and explored by

using the describer's or the pupil's body.

Independent exploration of objects
During description the person will independently explore the target. If it is difficult to receive or explore a target, for instance a cell of the body because of its small size or a part of plant because of its fragility, it is still possible sometimes to feel raised images or models of them when provided.

3.3 From wide description into details

Space has been defined as a location with a certain size, borders, quality and purpose connected to the certain location or part of the location (Nykysuomen sanakirja, 1959). Perceiving space and orientation are independent functions, which include the awareness of one's own location in the space, from where one has come from and where one can go to.

Description includes information connected to space, the basic form of the location and objects related to that. The concept "market place" often reminds us of a rectangular or square large space with sales' tables. "A shopping centre" as a construction consists of several floors, various shops and possibly escalators. "A cinema" includes rows of seats and a big screen on one end of the room. Basic concepts are often connected with the relationship of objects to each other (market place: straight sales table and walking lines, cinema: seat rows rising towards the back of the room). Concepts also include activities, order and special use related to the space. Usually there is written information somewhere in the space (name of employee, numbers, names of floors), signs and symbols (toilet, emergency exit, fire extinguisher). (Lahtinen, 2008a)

In detailed descriptions the main subjects are followed by the details. Description can also be classified according to the size of the space: general, physical, social or personal space. These can be divided into even more precise areas of description; description of extensive space, large space, room space, nearby space, social space, action and separate targets. Description of nearby space, social space and action can be related to the description of the changing situations and activities, description of a moving or changing target as well as description of deviations, risks and level differences. In addition to a stable space the described target (horse racing) or scenery (stars in the night sky) may move. The scenery may move, for instance seen from a train window. (e.g. Lahtinen et.al. 2006)

A general space is a wide space, which surrounds the person and to which he/she does not necessarily have a physical contact (scenery). Physical environment is a space where the person has experienced different properties of it, including for instance the amount of light, sounds (noise, silence) and objects. People have a tactile and/or other sensory physical experience of their environment. A sensory experience to a physical space may have been received for instance when orientating within that space. Social space includes people present in the space. The joint, shared space around the describer and the receiver in physical contact is called social body space. Personal space means the nearby space which can be touched. Spatial body space means a space experienced by the person to which he/she does not have a constant physical contact. This can, however, be touched with the body without moving e.g. to touch the wall and lamp by reaching out his/her hand. (Lahtinen, 2008a) Dimensions of the space are divided into distances (close, far), levels (above, below), places (in front of, behind) and sides of body (right, left). Some description methods from wide to detailed has been collected into figure 3.

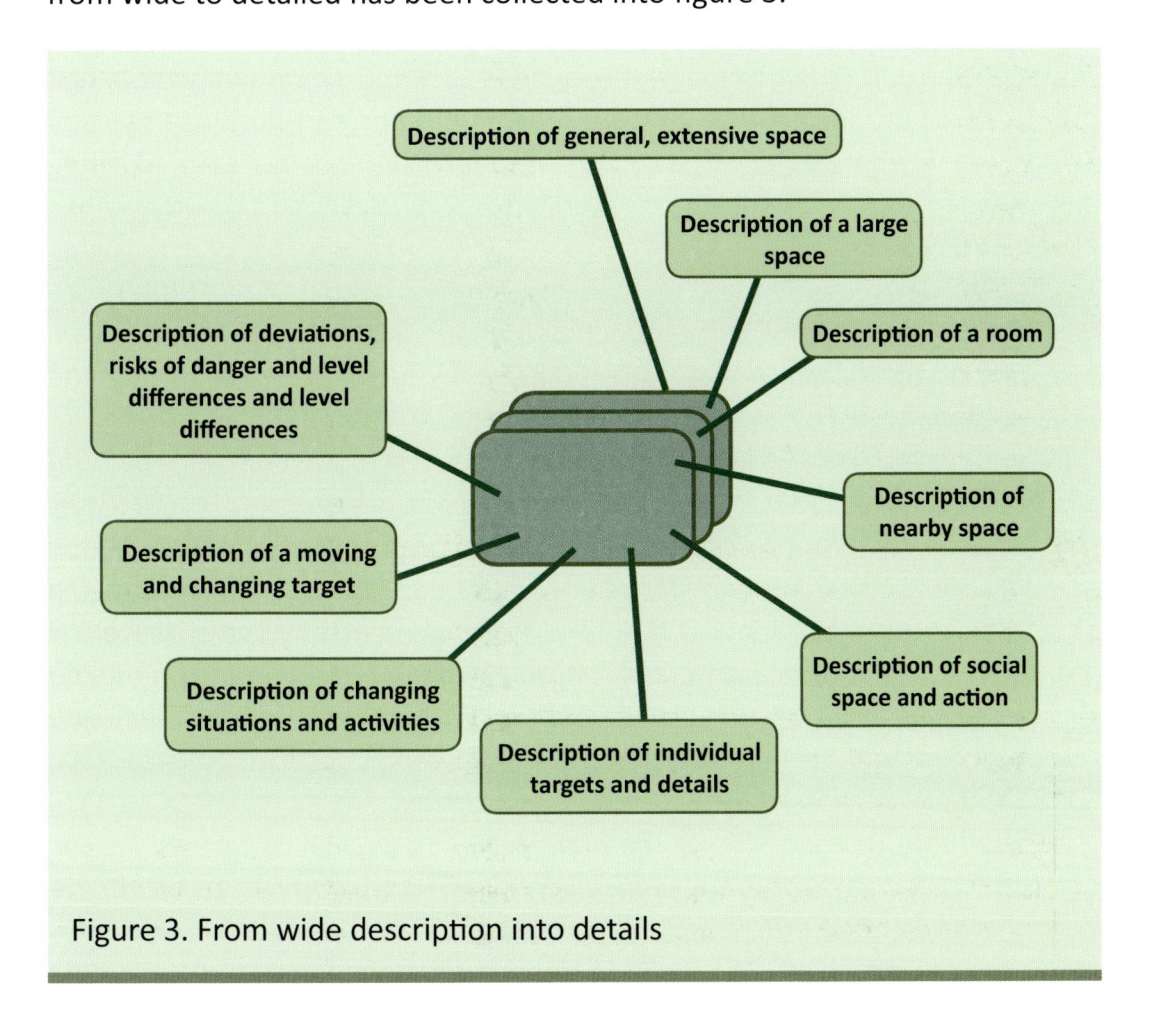

Figure 3. From wide description into details

Description of general, extensive space
This includes describing landscape and wide scenery. For instance when hiking, the description may include the surrounding landscape from the top of a mountain. On the train the description of wide space may mean description of landscape that is passing by. In a town or on a field trip you describe the environment and scenery to the pupils. At the market place you describe the form of a market and the position of different sales stands:

- *We are now in the corner of the square. The market place is rectangular. They sell flowers on the right hand stands. In the middle they sell cakes and vegetables. On the left there is a café.*

Description of large space
This is about describing space with touchable contours and into which you can go. These are spaces with various areas, rooms and corridors. Examples of extensive spaces are a railway station, a shopping centre, a museum, a church or a restaurant. On a school trip or excursion you can describe a new space like a swimming hall as follows:

"This swimming hall is a big rectangular space. You are by its long wall, like on the beach. A slope leads diagonally to the pool. We are at the shallow end. The swimming pool consists of three sections. There are water massage showers on the wall of the pool to the right. On the right hand side at 2 o'clock there is a circular island, where there is a jet water shower. There are steps up to the island. A pillar in the middle of the hall divides the swimming pool in two. To the front left hand side there is a wave pool. When moving right and forwards across the pool, there is a big circular shower pipeline in the roof giving water bubbles. On the left hand side in the middle of the pool there is a children's slide. When you move to that section, there is a small children's slide at 10 o'clock. At the third section there is a slide construction. The slide which reaches from the opposite side of the pool to this side gives you speed for the entire ride. It is for adults and children. You can swim in a track around the construction. It is a narrow upstream track. An adult can always stand on this pool. The walls of the swimming hall are windows facing

- outwards. At the bottom of the pool there is a blue line, which follows
- the constructions. At the moment there are adults and children at all
- sections."

Description of a room
You describe a space, where you act in a certain, foreseeable way i.e. it is a question of describing a functional space. The place is frequently used (craft room) or rarely (doctor's clinic):

- - *Right in front is the reception desk. The waiting area opens to the right*
- *with about 10 empty chairs on each side of the corridor. The doctor's*
- *door is the last door on the right. In the middle of the corridor there is*
- *a table on the left with magazines and drinking water.*

Describing nearby space i.e. personal space
Description of near space is related to exploring one's own place and work station (chair and table areas). At the shared morning session the class is told how pupils around the table are positioned and which objects are related to this session:

- - *Jane, Alan is sitting on your left hand side, then Susan and Peter. There*
- *is a book on the table and flowers in a vase.*

Description of social space and activities
People present in the social space are named and positioned. If the describer does not know the names of those in the group, he/she can tell their gender or provide other information (adult, child). Others present in this space are positioned for instance according to where they are sitting at the table. At a presentation the names of the people are placed to a drawn form of the table. This works for a meeting and in hobby situations. At a gathering the pupils are described before placement of the chairs, pupils present and objects relevant to the event:

- *The piano is next to the wall with the door. Seats are placed so that you face the piano and the windows are behind your back. Other musical instruments are between you and the piano.*

Description of individual targets and details

At museums and exhibitions you describe objects such as statues, paintings and images:

- *In this black and white photo there is a sauna by a river. A wide river is flowing in the foreground of the picture. The water is dark and there are waves on the surface. On the opposite bank of the river there are bushes and trees with leaves. On this bank there is a sauna hut, and smoke is coming from the chimney. In front of the sauna there is a dock on the beach.*

Description of changing situations and activities

When the order of pupils and objects has been changed in a class room, you describe the new situation to the pupils:

- *Some students have changed seats. John is sitting by the window wall in front. Julia is sitting behind John.*

Description of a moving and changing target

A space, landscape or target may change or move. Changing information is given for instance in a vehicle onto a neutral area of the body like the thigh of a person with visual impairment. With the touch message you position the departure and terminal station, where the orientation location is given by touch at each intermediate station. There will be changes in the target caused by movement (scenery from the window) in a vehicle:

- *We are stopping at a large shopping centre. On the left there is a big car park. Behind that is the shopping centre.*

Description of deviations, danger risks and level differences
At hotels or other comparable places you describe the position of the stairs, level differences, obstacles up and down so that the person can be prepared for them beforehand:

- *- The lift is opposite the reception. On the left of the lift there is a fleet of stairs both up to the floors and down to the dining room.*

Exercises and reflections

Classification of description

1. How do the classifications of description work when describing for an individual and for a group?

2. Which differences are brought into description situation by one-way verbal description, reciprocal language description and functional dialogue description?

Description of spaces

3. You travel by train with a person with visual impairment for the first time from home to a new meeting place in a different town. Think about what kinds of places you may have to describe during the journey.

4. You have arrived at a new three-floor shopping centre. What would you choose first to describe?

Drawing according to description

5. Draw a swimming pool hall according to the verbal description. Read the text aloud for others and compare your drawings. How do the drawings differ from each other?

"The swimming pool hall is a big rectangular space. We are near the short wall. The other three walls have window, which you can see out of. There are two swimming pools. The one in the front is a big pool for adults, in an S-shape and there are various water activities in different places. Behind the adult pool there is a round pool for children. You get to the pools on the right side. There are two separate stairs leading to the adult pool, and one to the children's pool.

The pool for adults is right in front of us and there is a semicircular upstream lane. There is room for 2-3 people to swim side by side. In the lower neck of the S-shape there is a larger centre of the pool and on its left edge there are stone steps. Water mass is flowing down the stones. At the beginning of the S there are several bubble spots at the bottom of the pool. People are standing on the bubble spots."

4 Description to various receivers

4.1 Description given to children and young people with visual impairment

Child's vocabulary, linguistic ability, background and experience influence the language and choices of lexicon during the description as well as how extensively or detailed you describe and which style is chosen. Receiving information demands concentration, so when you describe to a child/youth, you may have to leave some material out. At an art exhibition, is it necessary to describe every detail of everything to a pupil, or is it better to leave something out and focus on the essential? The aim of description is to support the studied subjects. It takes more time to describe and explore objects than to study them visually. Familiar vocabulary is used in description, although it is good to learn new terminology simultaneously in the authentic environment. One should never explain a new word with another new word. Description places certain demands on language. Which is the best method of describing to a visually impaired child whether something is "in front of" or "behind"? Does "in front of the door" mean indoors or outside the building? During description it is good to once in a while to check the child/youth has understood.

Description is bound to a certain time, space and event. When describing to a child/youth, you should also pay attention to the intonation, tempo and pitch of your voice. Your voice should support the description and not be contradictory. You should be aware of the possible use of dialect and various cultural issues in your choice of vocabulary. In addition, you have to think about how to use evaluating attributes (handsome) or adjectives (narrow, big) in determining geometric relations. Which words are neutral? Which words create an atmosphere? Do you need to be able to repeat a description, when the target group consists of children, youth or adults? Should you only describe what you see, or are you allowed to interpret, for instance by including your own feelings in the description? It is important, that the child/youth receives a personal experience and sensation. The child/youth could be involved in the description from the start so he receives some training.

A partially sighted pupil in Year 9 with perception difficulties described a dog called Mökä as he wanted the dog to be described (picture 4):

Picture 4. Mökä in a sweater

- *"This is a picture of a dachshund. It is covered from neck to tail by a sweater.*
- *It is on a lead. It is winter. The dog is light brown. Parts of its tail are little*
- *darker. The sweater is colourful and covers most of the front paws."*

A concrete target of exploration (raised image, object) accompanied with description helps the child/youth to concentrate and makes them able to receive a description. It helps them perceive and understand size, proportions and distance (embossed map of the route should be learnt). A felt object will concretely expose the multidimensionality of the target, which otherwise may be difficult for the child/youth to perceive. When possible, you should always use a concrete model (a real coin when learning about money) or a touchable piece of art when describing to a child/youth. In gymnastic exercises the pupil is helped to move or the describer moves with the pupil. It is demanding to receive purely auditory descriptions. Handling (materials used in art classes) and understanding of description (embossed map in studying continents) are something that has to be learned consciously and consistently with the pupil. These abilities are not innate but trained. By training these skills pupils will learn to understand more about the surrounding visual world. According to Honkanen & Vartio (1998) children born blind need support in order to build up their mental images. The imagination of a child with visual impairment needs stimuli and conscious supervision provided by adults.

In a teaching situation it is essential to learn the matter, and description supports this goal. When you are practising a mathematic diagram and how to read it with a pupil, it is good to have a clear example as a description target. If the pupil commands the diagram well, you can advance into more specific and minute details. "The basic meaning and value of a certain symbolic message can be fully understood only in the framework of 'the language' which it has been created with. There is no completely corresponding verbal translation for a mathematical formula." (Salminen, 2005, 40) In the following examples mathematical diagrams are described to a pupil:

Height growth as a function of age

- Height growth of people in different ages is described with x/y-coordinate system as a function of age. Ages on x-axis are 5, 10 and 15 years. On the y-axis there are heights 1 m, 1,50 m and 1,70 m. The plot shows the average height of people in different ages. It shows that the average height of a 5-year-old is 1 m, 10-year-old 1,50 m and 15-year-old 1,70 m.

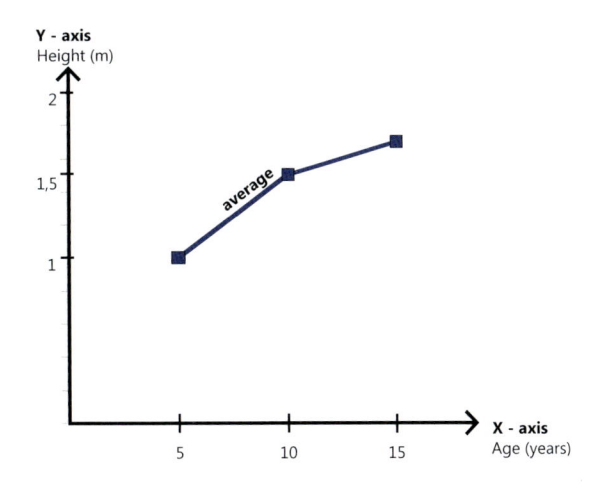

The description will progress as follows:

You tell the subject about the plot graph. In description you first go through the concepts; m, yrs, average, x- and y-axis. You draw and name the axis on the pupil's hand, palm or back.

By drawing lines you add ages along x-axis and heights along y-axis.

You add the diagram the plot of the function, draw and describe how it advances as well as what the main contents are.

For example: A finger at the beginning of the function plot: Aged 5 the average height is 1 m (point 5 yrs on x-axis and 1 m on y-axis). A line is drawn the next point: At 10 the average height is 1,50 m (point 10 yrs on x-axis and 1,50 m on y-axis). A line is drawn to the next point: At 15 the average height is 1,70 m (point 15 yrs on x-axis and 1,70 m on y-axis). Describe the diagram again verbally and by drawing. Support the learning by giving the pupil a raised image too.

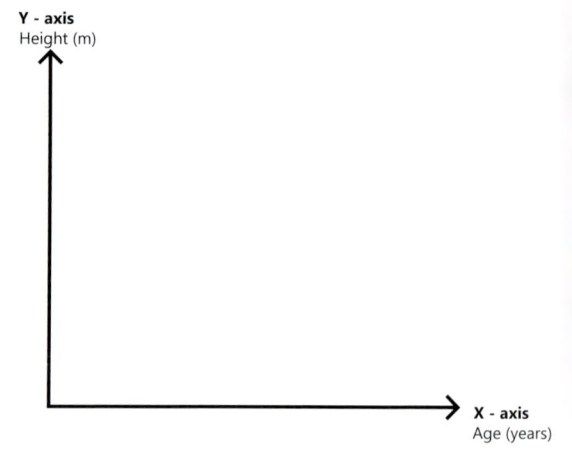

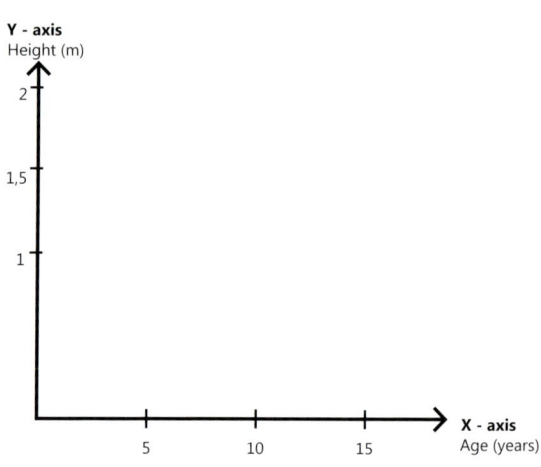

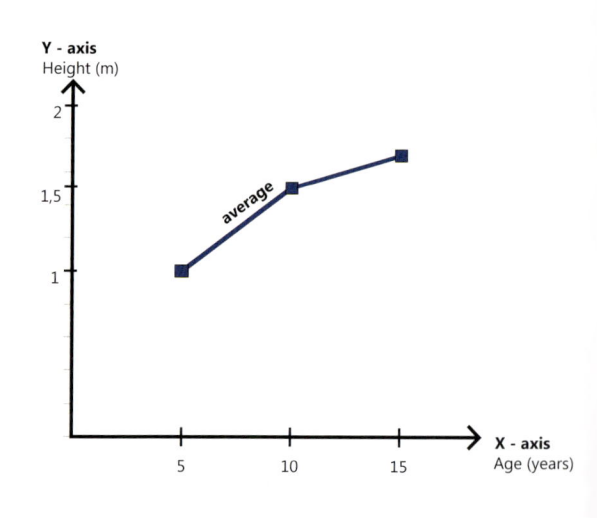

20 % of the population has a dog

20 % of the population is shown on a pie chart. The whole pie chart represents 100 % i.e. the total population. It is divided into four equal sections. Each one is 25 % of the population. 20 % is less than 25 %.

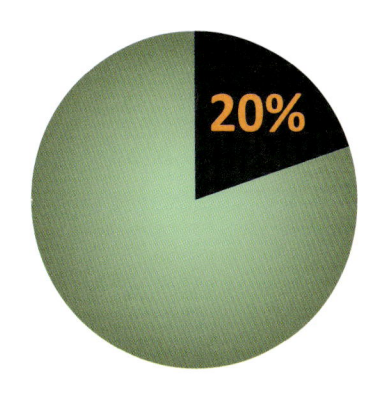

This is how description progresses:
First you talk about the subject. If you are using a raised image, the pupil can explore the model while the description takes place. Draw onto the back while describing. It is easier to understand percentages, if you explain 100 %, 50 % and 25 % of the pie chart first.

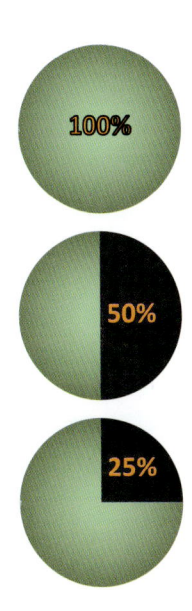

A 20 % sector is drawn in the pie chart.

Describe it again and draw on the back as well as explore a raised image.

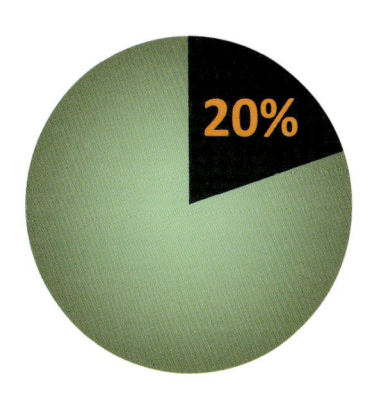

Describing a classroom

When starting at school all the relevant locations are described to a new pupil. Describing his classroom makes it possible for the pupil to move and study more independently. All pupils will benefit from the description. Start with naming the walls then carry on with other details. Give the student enough time to get acquainted with his classroom. Be consistent and repetitive with a visually impaired pupil and give them time. The following example describes Jack's background and how he acquainted himself with his classroom:

- Jack is a junior pupil. He is blind and has cerebral palsy. Jack has perception difficulties and the left hand side of his body is spastic i.e. the muscle tone is too high. He needs a lot of adult support, his ability to move and explore is minimal. Description supports Jack's daily. Familiar concepts are used. Jack's aim is to be as independent as possible. When he is familiar with his classroom, he has more time to study, and knows where objects are and can orientate himself. Description of the landmarks helps Jack to perceive his environment. First relevant information is described and drawn onto Jack's back taking safety into consideration.

- *"The classroom is rectangular. The door-wall has a door in it. The door opens into the corridor. The blackboard-wall is on the right. At the opposite side of the door-wall there is the window-wall. On the opposite wall to the blackboard-wall are the lockers. To the right of the door is a corner with a rubbish bin, sink and blackboard. There are windows along the whole length of the window-wall. There are four big cupboards by the cupboards-wall. Your books are in the two cupboards next to the window, Jack. By the door-wall there are two shelves close to the door..."*

- *After exploring the classroom they recall the location of objects. At the same time the classroom, objects in it and route to Jack's own desk are drawn onto his back. The description is repeated if necessary and details are added according to the pupil's interest and needs. If there is a miniature or raised image, it supports the description.*

4.2 Audio description as service for people with visual impairment

Audio description allows access to various cultural services. Audio description is a service form addressed to a client with visual impairment, giving a verbal description of visual targets in cultural events (i.e. www.audiodescribe.com; www.rnib.org.uk; www.vocaleyes.co.uk). Audio description existed in the USA since in 1970's and its use expanded in 1980's. In England many movies and theatres have been audio described for years. In Finland audio description is also used and audio description equipment can be borrowed from Cultural Service for the Visually Impaired (CSVI). "A ghost voice" whispers to a microphone during silences in a play describing the facial expressions and gestures of actors, scene and costumes. (Mäkinen-Vuohelainen, 2009; Turunen, 2008)

In different countries audio description has different names. In Sweden the concept is "syntolkning" ("visual interpreter"), when they describe plays and musicals through earphones at the theatre (Pehrson, 2000). In Swedish "syntolk" is a person who describes the scene with speech as well as landscapes, setting i.e. things that the person with visual impairment cannot see and this causes difficulty in following the events (Nimpuno, 1995). The describer can be physically in a different room, when his/her speech will not disturb the audience.

In Finland for instance art exhibitions, theatre performances, movies and competitions have been audio described. There are pre-recorded audio described targets for instance at exhibitions and museums, which can be heard through earphones (Nilsson, 1997). "Kuunneltuja kuvia" (Listened images) (Othman, 1987) was produced in Ateneum art museum as one of the first described art materials. This includes pre-recorded descriptions of paintings as well as raised images. The pre-recording includes certain chosen sound landscapes in addition to description itself. Explanations of visual information were produced by preparing and recording beforehand for a project called "Kuvia korville" (Images for ears). The explanations benefit the museum's customers with visual impairment. The recording includes more description than a normal guided tour. The particular room including the pieces of art in there are explained. (Voutilainen, 2001)

CSVI organized the first education of audio description in autumn 2005. The education that was supported by the Ministry of Education lasted for 64 hours. Up to 2009 two groups of describers have been trained. They described cultural events, visual arts, theatre and cinema. (Turunen, 2005)

Getting describers to various events is still disorganised and is mostly based on voluntary work in Finland. The contents of holistic audio description still require further studies. Often the describers of visual targets are employees of various art institutions, so they include artists' personal working history, genres and typical features of their eras as well as social and political changes in their descriptions. Today audio description for a person with visual impairment consists of visual description of a performance, an event or a piece of art. Description may even be printed. Parts of description are produced for theatre performances, movies, cultural events and visual arts (Mäkinen-Vuohelainen, 2008).

4.3 Description in everyday life of people with dual sensory impairment and deafblindness

A person with deafblindness may be profoundly deaf and blind or he/she may have functional hearing and/or sight, in which case he/she will be able to use their residual senses to the maximum when receiving a description. People with deafblindness receive description through speech, sign language and/or other methods. A hearing aid wearer uses either a personal radio microphone or room loop system in noisy situation. In that case the describer will talk into a microphone and the receiver's hearing aid is set to "T" position. The receiver will hear only what is said into the microphone, but not the reactions of the audience.

It is demanding for a person with deafblindness to receive description, because it is made with the same sense of touch he/she uses as a communication channel. In other words, environmental description is a part of communication. He/she will be described the events in the environment; who are present, who is talking, who enters or leaves and when it is his/her turn to speak. Description makes it possible to receive in real time information of people's words, reactions and emotions. Socially there are changes happening; people speak fast and events change continually. Participation and interaction are increased by a direct contact with the environment and objects. People's hands tell about their feelings and reactions in direct contact. You can feel interest, tenseness, excitement, relaxedness and laughing from the hands. It is not always possible to transfer the information in real time, in which case it can be given afterwards. With postponed description you can add the guest speaker's clothing and hair style and other details.

With the help of sufficient description a deafblind person can feel safe, independent and able to participate in making choices. He/she can enjoy being involved in the situation and be interested in the experience. Through practical exercises description will become more functional and precise. Description informs about new and special issues as well as so called unexpressed changes in social situations, manners and reactions. It is fundamental for contacting other people. The basic description rises from information picked up by the person with deafblindness, and it supports the person's own experiences. Systematic information provided by description will give a general picture of the target. It will also give a hint of future events. When describing a new matter, a more precise and detailed description is needed. (e.g. Raanes, 2004; Smith, 1994)

Description as a part of interpretation situation
In addition to translating language and guiding, interpreting for a person with deafblindness includes environmental description and the different methods (Lahtinen, 2004). According to the Interpretation service manual for the deafblind (Lahtinen, 2006) description is divided into description of environment, space and action. Then the visual (what is seen) and auditory (what is heard) information as well as information related to other senses is transmitted to the receiver either verbally (spoken, signed, written) or non-verbally (e.g. pointing at target, drawing onto body, haptices). When it comes to the deafblind or dual sensory impaired, the description is part of their general or personal interpretation. Description to a group is often spoken into a loop microphone, when all users of the loop system can hear the description at the same time. If a person is listening through a loop and in addition has a personal interpreter, the interpreter can transmit the pieces of information, which are not conveyed by the loop. This may be information on changes and atmosphere of the situation.

While a person with deafblindness is interacting with another person through an interpreter, he/she may express to the interpreter, that he/she is interested in the discussion partner's tone of voice, movements of signing or eye contact, and then the interpreter must transmit these facts. Behaviour is described in context and usually in real time. It is important, that the interpreter can transmit the reactions of the discussion partners, such as laughing, seriousness, interest or in a hurry. (Jakeŝ, 2003; Reyes, 1996)

In various cultural events people with deafblindness receive information through a sign language interpreter. When a person with deafblindness and his/her interpreter are aware of various alternatives of communication, the receiver can participate more. A sign language interpreter can explain visual information about a painting through language. How is it possible to share message given by the picture and to empathise with it? How can we make the painting come an alive and be a shared experience? You can draw it with the customer into the air, onto the back or make it together into a 3-D painting using movements. There are people who only want verbal or signed explanation, and this wish should be respected. An interpreter may offer various alternatives of which the customer chooses appropriative ones and may suggest methods suitable for him/herself.

Hobbies are related with description of other people's actions. To transmit this information is of special importance for people with deafblindness. For instance in addition to the description of actors and setting at a theatre, you describe the reactions of other people, such as applause. The describer may then through a bodily message give information of the applauding by clapping onto a shoulder or on an arm. Then the receiver can join in with the same action in real time if he/she so wishes (picture 5). The touch showing applause gives information on the actions and feelings of other people; starting, duration and ending of the applause as well as its intensity, rhythm and speed. Intensity, rhythm and changes in speed are experienced as qualities connected with emotion. (Lahtinen, 2008a, 99-100)

Picture 5. Showing applause onto a body

Description quarter

A description quarter has been used at events and meetings of Finnish Deafblind Association. The description quarter means a prepared description, the aim of which is to give a brief and concise verbal description of the location at the beginning of the meeting. During this initial description the parts and special areas of the location are named clearly into the loop. Information of description quarter was published in a Finnish newsletter for people with deafblindness (Lahtinen, 2003a, 17):

> *"Interpreting and understanding of it will be easier, if you get acquainted with the room in advance. This can be done independently before the event starts or with an interpreter. You arrive at the place of interpretation early – which is why it is the named description quarter. Description quarter is a part of an interpretation situation. It is the conscious description of location, activities, people and objects, getting to know them before the actual event starts.*
>
> *The length of a description quarter depends on the deafblind person's wishes. Sometimes five minutes can be enough, another time you may need half an hour to familiarise yourself. When the description quarter is before the event, make sure you allow enough time for it.*
>
> *It is an advantage to get familiar with the place. If the person with deafblindness already knows the size of the room, place of the speaker etc., it is easier for him/her to choose his/her seat. Sometimes there may be nice surprises in a room, which you will not find, unless you have time to get to know them. For some people getting to know the place gives an opportunity for independent orientation. It is easier, when you know which obstacles there are and where they are.*
>
> *It is beneficial to know about the environment beforehand, especially if the place is challenging in terms of interpretation. When you are going to a spa, you can go around the premises in advance, and get an idea of what to expect of the pools (bubbles under your feet, outdoor pool). This is necessary especially if the deafblind person does not know tactile methods or tactile signing, and it is impossible to hear in the pool.*

> It is the person with deafblindness who selects the methods of environmental description. The options are: independent orientation, interpretation with spoken/sign language or guiding the hand to explore objects. These can be combined with other methods, such as drawing onto hand/palm, surface of table or back. It is most important to have enough time for the description quarter. You can then achieve the most."

Description related to a meeting is divided into four parts; preparing/advance description, description quarter, description during the meeting and postponed description. Preparing includes agreeing the progress and rhythm of description together with the chairman and organisers. The describer's place, timing and description of certain situations, such as voting are agreed on. By doing this you can avoid overlapping speeches. Description starts as agreed.

Advance description includes making a basic map of the meeting location. In the map there are named walls, places of seats and basic lines as well as relevant targets for following actions and issues. The map can be studied beforehand, so that everyone has an opportunity to the use same names of targets in the room. The map is visible to all, perhaps near the door. Personal interpreters can use information on the map to support their interpretation and drawing. Description of the room is divided into general information on the shape of the room and naming the walls as well as specialities of the location and place of general interpreters:

> "On the right hand side by the door-wall there are two lottery tables full of prizes. Beyond the tables there is a coat rack and a computer table. Behind the chairman's table beside the window-wall there is a place for a general sign language interpreter and on the door-wall side there is an interpreter for signed Finnish."

During the meeting, for instance all visitors are described; numbers of those present as well as people moving and reasons for silence are mentioned. A presentation round can be made for example in sitting order, which gives a mental image of the size of the room and location of people simultaneously. In small meeting situations the presentation round will be made according the order of people around the table. Often at a meeting you ask for the floor with showing the number tags, which are distributed beforehand. The requests of floor can be expressed in different ways. The chairman's personal interpreter may express them to him/her, who repeats information into a microphone. One way is to use a describer:

- *Chairman: "Have others requested the floor?"*
- *The chairman's personal interpreter gives information on requests for the floor by expressing with social quick message that a hand is up.*
- *Describer: "There are no hands up at the moment …In the middle of the hall no 21 stands up."*

When the describer speaks for the first time, she can tell her name ("The describer is Tina."). The beginning of description can be expressed using the word "description". When the meeting goes on after a break, the describer can tell how many people there are in the hall and how the communication situation works. During the meeting, officials change places. Here is an example of a chairman changing:

- *Describer: "Description. Mr Long rises and walks to the chairman's table. The chairman Mrs Short rises. They hug. Managing director Mr Big shakes hands with Mr Long. Mr Long takes his seat behind the table. To the left of him there is an interpreter. Mrs Short leaves the row of seats on the door side. Mr Long is given a wireless microphone which he attaches to his collar."*

Description adds a dimension. Before the event it is good for the deafblind person to discuss his/her wishes about interpretation. Sometimes a person with deafblindness has two interpreters, which gives the possibility for one of them to concentrate on language interpretation and the other on environmental description as agreed beforehand.

4.4 Describing the auditory world to a person with hearing impairment

The auditory world is described to a person with hearing impairment. The receiver may be hard of hearing, deafened or profoundly deaf. He/she may use various hearing devices (hearing aids, cochlear implant, radio microphone, loop system etc.). The person may also be visual impaired. Description can be produced by speaking, writing (speech-to-text / palantype interpreter) or sign language (visual, tactile). For a person using a cochlear implant new and weird sounds need a name when learning new sounds. Sounds are usually described in sound sensations (machines, clinking cups, mobile phone, door bell), sounds of nature (rain, thunder), human voices (sniffly, loud) and animal sounds (purring cat, barking dog).

The source of the sound is named when describing a sound. Typical sounds are human voices (man, woman, child), sounds of nature (sea, water, wind), animal sounds (singing birds, sounds of insects), functional sounds (loudspeaker, skate board) and alarm signals (ambulance, fire engine) as well as sounds of materials (paper, stone, wood, plastic). Perceiving a sound is connected with locating it (indoor or outdoor). There are various elements of a sound, such as the beginning and end, its intensity (silent, moderate, loud), quality and/or duration (short-long, even-uneven), direction and approximate distance from the listener, position of the sound source in relation to the listener and whether it moves or stays still. A snow plough's warning signal in a guiding situation outdoors with a person with hearing impairment follows:

- *- It starts and ends: it is a repeated warning signal when the snow plough is reversing. The sound is high-pitched and loud.*

In subtitling programmes visual text description of voices is used. In the United Kingdom they use colour in subtitles to illustrate different speakers (white, yellow, blue, green). In addition, the subtitles note in brackets reactions of actors (yelling, whistling), tones (hissing) and environmental tones/sound sources (train, knock at door, school bell, car horn, dog barking, telephone ringing). The tones of the speaker's voice are put in brackets, such as whispering. The music style (dance music, rave music), composer and name of the piece (Mozart's Clarinet concerto) are mentioned.

Exercises and reflections

Description to various receivers

1. What are the differences in describing to a child or an adult?

2. Reflect on the meaning of description for people who are partially sighted, profoundly blind or deafblind.

3. What is the difference between description for the profoundly blind or for the acquired blind person?

4. Which specific characteristics do deafness bring to a description situation?

Environmental sources of sound

5. Concentrate on listening to environmental sounds with your eyes closed. Name the sources of sound you hear and how far they are away.

5 Description in different situations

Targets of description in different situations have been chosen from everyday social activities in various places, extensive environments and arts. The surrounding flow of information may briefly make the describer speechless and many questions spin in his/her mind; what should you describe to a person when you go into a market hall? Has he/she been there before? Is the place familiar? Which targets are the receivers interested in? If it is a familiar place, you should add new information. The person may have a special reason to visit the market hall; he/she may want to buy fresh fish for example.

5.1 Description of people and their behaviour

Description of people
Description of people can be divided into describing oneself and describing another person. When describing another person it may be challenging to find neutral expressions to some things, such as estimating body structure and age when others are listening. When you describe yourself, you can choose what you want to express to others and the concepts with which you want to describe yourself. When describing yourself, you usually describe your height, age, body shape, hair colour (light, dark, brown or blonde), length and style (shoulder length, a bob, with fringe or a side parting, crimped or pony tail), hair jewellery (clip, hair band), clothes (colours, style), details (ear rings, rings, glasses or piercings), job and where you come from. The two last things cannot be seen by anyone. People with a dual sensory impairment will usually tell you their method of communication:

- - *I am a 170 cm (5 ft 7 in) tall, well-proportioned woman. I have long brown hair down to my hips, which is up in a bun. I wear glasses. I am wearing a dark green suit and long necklace with red felted pearls and black leather slippers with a small green bow. I am 45-years old and*

- *use sign language.*

Description of clothes includes the names and type of clothing worn. Don't forget to describe shoes and jewellery. The following example is a description the dress worn by a doctoral candidate (Ristimäki, 2008):

- *She is wearing a suit with an ankle-length skirt. It is a dark grey wool fabric; with a letter H here and there pattern in silver black thread. The blouse has Cossack style sleeves with eyelet-buttons and slits on the sleeves which reveal a black satin cloth. There is a stand-up collar at the back of her neck changing into a mandarin collar at the front. Also at the front of the suit there are eyelet-buttons.*

It is a good idea to ask the target of description in advance, how he/she would like to be described. The description has to match the type of event. At the beginning of a jubilee ceremony it does not sound correct and tactful to describe the mayor as "a bald 60-year-old man with a large stomach", even if everyone else can see that! Usually you only describe gender, estimated age and height, body shape, style of clothes and then add other details where appropriate.

- *Mr Brown is around 50 years old, 180 cm (6 ft) tall and muscular. He is wearing a light short sleeved brown silk shirt with a dark brown stand-up collar. His trousers are light and he is wearing brown polished leather shoes. On his right wrist he has a thick golden bracelet. He has dark, straight, shoulder-long hair, which is tied back with a brown velvet ribbon.*

Sometimes people describe with words that can feel insulting (skinny/anorexic, a drug addict or junkie). The description gets more difficult, if you are not familiar with concepts illustrating the target (rasta hair, crimped). Body structure is usually described with concepts like normal, well-proportioned, strong, chubby or thin. When it comes to height, the concepts short or tall are used. Face shapes may be round or oval. Hair colour may be for instance medium brown, sand brown or blond. Age can be described by saying that he/she is about 50-60 years of age or that she is clearly older than him in the picture or by stating that he/she is retired. About style of clothes you first describe the outfit (evening dress, lounge suit), model (strapless evening dress), colour and details ("The dress is plain and has a v-shaped collar."). Use body parts to describe clothes´ patterns or pockets etc. ("There is a thick white stripe on the chest of the sweater and its hem is below the knee.")

Description of behaviour
In interaction you observe behaviour and non-verbal communication. Behaviour and facial expressions can be described. Those include for instance tones of voice and style of signing (speed, pauses, expressions), facial expressions (smile, yawn) and glances (eye contact, wandering gaze), movement (fast, exaggeratingly slow), body positions (standing tall, sitting relaxed), behaviour (polite or rude) and distance between people (side by side, opposite one another at a table). Non-verbal communication is heard (pitch, stress and tone of voice), seen (mime, gesture, movement, position, distance, occupying the space) or conveyed by touch.

For a person with visual impairment environmental description offers an opportunity to receive information also on reactions he/she cannot see or hear. When you are aware of how the other person within conversation behaves, you can respond to it in numerous, relevant ways; by smiling or by showing you are listening by turning to the speaker.

A face gives away lots of information. When communicating eyes usually focus on the other person's face. The describer follows the glance of a speaker or signer and describes it. He/she can explain the direction, duration and intensiveness of the glance. Description of facial expressions may be made with the help of the so called emotional response hand (picture 6) presented by Lahtinen (2008a, 62). Touch messages convey one's own state and feelings, and at the same time the facial expressions of other people. Common facial expressions are described while conversing on agreed parts of the body, such as onto the hand, back or shoulder.

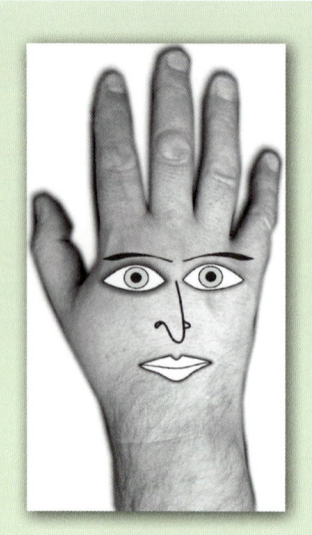

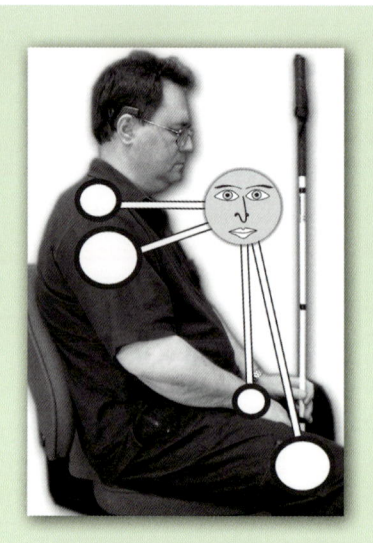

Picture 6. Emotional response hand and different parts of the body

You can describe facial expressions like laughing, not reacting, corners of the mouth down or wet eyes and tears. When you are used to receiving facial information through the emotional response hand, your sensitivity to receive touch and movements will develop. In time the number of lexicon of different messages may grow (falling to sleep, waking up, yawning). In addition, there may be some physiological changes on the face, such as blushing and sweating. The head may nod (yes-message) or move from side to side (no-message). You can feedback using voice, such as "hmm" or "yeah" sounds. With movements you describe the discussion partner's position in the situation; is he/she standing, sitting or changing his/her feet all the time. The describer cannot interpret another person's emotional state but she/he has to rely on what she/he sees: It is the receiver's responsibility to specify from the target of description how he/she feels by asking appropriate questions.

5.2 Description of new internal space

When you enter public buildings there is usually a sign on the door with the name and/or location of the room. If the room or locations are unnamed, a general name has to be provided (class room, office). Description is begun by naming the walls on entrance into the room. Naming is based on the wall's function (door-wall) or touchable surface, design or material (window-wall, bay-window-wall, brick-wall). Include description of the furniture, safe routes for moving around at the location, as well as if the room is cramped or wide. The order of tables and seats is described with basic forms ("The chairs are in a U-shape."). When the location has been described, the receiver can perceive it more precisely by moving within it. Exploring on one's own gives more detailed information about the space holistically, the location of objects, materials, distances, proportions and relations of various objects to each other (i.e. Smith, 1994).

A person with visual impairment may get acquainted with new premises alone or with a guide. Description may happen simultaneously as guiding. If a person uses tactile sign language, you often stop during description. When getting acquainted with the location together, the person with visual impairment may ask questions (Törrönen & Onnela, 1999). Going around a room can be done with a guiding grip usually along walls and by using the guide's leading hand. The leading hand points out objects to be explored. Point out the direction of the lights (natural light from the window, ceiling and wall lights). It is agreed with the receiver, how precisely the location is described.

In description it is good to show reflecting surfaces (mirror, window) when needed. They may dazzle or give wrong information about the size of the location (risk to bump into). When there are changes of direction in the room, level changes (stairs) or upper/lower obstacles you can bump into, they must be described. It is also advisable to mention the placement of fragile and sharp objects (knives on the table). The location is described with everyday concepts. Concepts used in description and perception are summarised as follows (i.e. Lahtinen, 2000; Törrönen & Lumiste, 1999):

1) naming the space: kitchen, hall, class room, auditorium, gym, meeting room
2) pointing out the orientation point: a touchable marker beside the door
3) the shape of room: square, rectangular, L-shaped, circle, straight, semi-circular
4) size of the room: in metres or in feet (6,5 ft width and 9,8 ft long) or in square feet (97 square ft)
5) the position of the door: location, other doors
6) naming the walls: door-wall, window-wall, cupboard-wall, board/painting-wall
7) objects along the sides and in the middle of the room: location, number, layout of the furniture
8) upper and lower obstacles and safety factors: low doorway or ceiling, steps, fragile objects
9) other people present: how many, who they are and what they do
10) walking around the room: by oneself or together with a guide.

The following example is a description based on previous facts of the so called Frans Leijon -meeting room at the Finnish Deafblind Association:

"This is the Frans Leijon -meeting room. Outside the door on the left-hand side above the name there is a picture of deafblind Frans Leijon. The room is rectangular. We are on the right hand corner of the short wall. The size of the room is about 17 x 20 feet (5 x 6 meters). On the right hand side there is a photo-wall, on the opposite of us there is a window and balcony-wall. On the left side there is a television, screen-wall and the door-wall is behind us. In the middle of the room there is an oval table filling almost the entire room. There are about 14 chairs around it. You can walk around the table. The passage is very narrow. There are not any other people in the room.

On the photo-wall there are three black and white photos of Frans Leijon. In the middle of the window and balcony-wall there is a door to a big balcony. It is empty. When entering the balcony you have to go over a high door step. In the left corner of the room there is an old desk, on

> *which there is induction loop system and a television. On the door-wall there is a big window with a view of the corridor. Now there are wooden blinds drawn down the window. From the ceiling over the table there are three microphones and a long lamp hanging downwards. Because they are high up, there is no risk of hitting one's head. There are coffee cups and water glasses on the table."*

When describing a space you can start nearby or far away from the receiver. Many receivers prefer a location to be described starting close by and moving outwards, so they can simultaneously make a mental map of the space. A person with visual impairment moves into a space using certain learnt routes. If the description of space starts from the door, the person will move from the target a-b-c-d. If the description of target continues from b to c, then the description of space is the same as the route. If you start another way around (d-c-b-a) he/she has to turn the map around in his/her mind. On the other hand, if the person has a narrow vision field, he/she may prefer to look at target by the door. It is difficult to perceive the close environment with a small vision field. Objects which are further away will appear more holistically in view. The situation may be helped by lighting so, that the person can use his/her functional residual vision as much as possible. Then he/she can ask about the targets they can see. The describer then proceeds using this information. Perceiving a certain space, information provided by other senses is used, for instance a breeze can be felt from a door or a window, a warm airstream from a fireplace and an echo helps us guess the size of the room.

Description of the hall at the University of Helsinki (picture 7) (Ristimäki, 2008):

> *"The hall is fan-shaped. Light cream entrance doors are located on the lower part of the fan, at both corners of the door-wall. About half a meter above the doors there are round and gold wall clocks. On the upper part of the door-wall along its whole length there is a two metre wide, empty balcony.*
>
> *When entering the hall there is a statue-wall on the left and a Galileo-wall on the right. The hall gets wider towards the back i.e. window-wall. The*

auditorium is rising. There are about dozen arched, greenish grey rows of seats. There are stairs on both sides of the seats and in the middle.

The lower part of the walls of the hall is light green and the upper part is white. The upper and lower parts are separated with a border with leaf-like patterns and gold-shade effects. On the statue-wall, in front of the space there are words Archimedes and Newton side by side written in embossed letters. Respectively, on the Galileo-wall, in front of the space, there are Maxwell and Galileo with embossed letters on the border. On the statue-wall and Galileo-wall there are windows at the far end.

In the front of the hall along the door-wall there is a podium. There is a robust, reddish brown wooden table on the podium. The table is about 1,5 m (5 ft) high and, and there are five spot lights above it. Beside the table on the side of Galileo-wall there is a reddish-brown speaker's podium."

Picture 7. The Hall

During description you can draw a map onto the receiver's body. A drawn map allows the receiver to build up a mental image of the target. You can draw onto a back or hand, this helps perception. On the hand you can locate targets even if you cannot sign. You can draw in the beginning and/or end of the description. In the end you can even draw the route you were using. The describer can practise by drawing a map on a piece of paper, where the most important targets of the space are located and named. The following example is about a brief general description of a meeting room, where the person with visual impairment is already seated and an introduction to the room has already been given (figure 4):

- *"We are sitting at a square shape table. There are two chairs on each*
- *side. You (X) are by the door-wall. On your left hand side is Lena. By the*
- *cupboard-wall on the left are Sean and Tim. By the window-wall opposite*
- *there are Alan and Maria. By the board-wall are Sally and Kathy. On the*
- *corner of the board-wall and window-wall there is a coffee table buffet*
- *with buns. The door to the toilet is in the corner of the cupboard-wall and*
- *window-wall."*

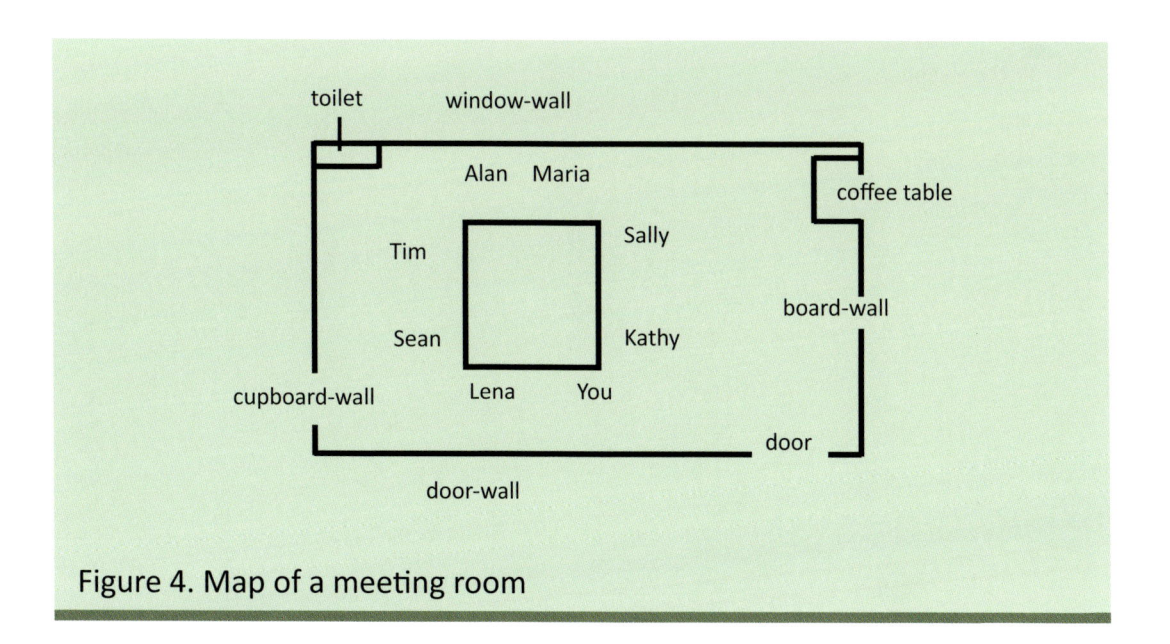

Figure 4. Map of a meeting room

If the receiver visits a place only once, he/she may suggest, that there is no need for description. If you are in a hurry and the meeting has already started, there is no time to describe the room. A solution for a quick description of a room might be telling only the basic facts of the room (people present, vacant and occupied seats, specialities and safety factors). For instance describing the room when having taken a blood sample at a health care centre:

- *A small room, with a high-back arm chair opposite the nurse's chair. There is a pillow on the chair. A laboratory trolley with glass tubes is located on the right of the chair. There is no-one in the room.*

The deafblind Helen Keller describes how she experienced a new space when getting to know a new location and house as follows (Freeman, 193, 76):

"In other people's houses, Helen notes "I can touch only what is shown to me - the chief objects of interest, carvings on the wall, or a curious architectural feature, exhibited like a family album". A house with which she is unfamiliar, therefore has at first no general effect or harmony of detail. It is not a complete conception, but a collection of object impressions, which as they come to me, are disconnected and isolated. But my mind, she explains, is full of associations, sensations, theories and with them I construct the house."

5.3 Describing landscape, architecture and buildings

Environment can be a natural scenic landscape or a man-made cultural landscape. It consists of different materials, architecture, styles (Gothic) and history. Today's architectural designs are visible in a landscape. It can be studied from different perspectives; biologic, temporal, human or structural landscapes. It keeps changing all the time (scenery of a city, countryside), while constructing new technology (wind power turbins). Rock foundation, soil, climate, waters, flora or fauna can be described. Dwellings and communication networks are examples of cultural markers (Rakennusperintömme, 2003).

Scenery is changing round the clock and every season. In scenery you can find geometry, contrasts, lights and shadows, similarities, repetitions, symmetry, asymmetry, curving lines, colours and patterns. (Waite, 1999) Describing the scenery can be thought of as a physical environment, which can be made more concrete by using various clues to distance and other illustrating expressions. In description it is possible to use either an active or passive sentence structure.

Active: - We are looking at a lake. The opposite shore is about 200 m (656 ft) from us. Willow herbs are growing in front of us together with other summer crops which are waist high.

Passive: - There is a view of lake landscape opening from the window. The distance to the opposite shore is about 200 m (656 ft). There are willow herbs and other summer crops up to waist-height growing behind the window.

When describing a building you name the target (block of flats), say how many floors there are (five floors), size (three stairways) and other details (glazed balcony). The building becomes more interesting when you describe details. "A day as tactile" –text (Lahtinen, 2003b) shows how a manor house estate can be described by an interpreter. If the person has never been to the estate, it will not necessarily differ at all from an ordinary big house to him/her. The receiver asked for a tactile experience of the manor house, which would give him a more concrete message of typical elements of the estate. The describer pointed out tall columns standing on both sides of the main entrance. By feeling the columns, their cold, plain stone material was perceived. This way the receiver could create a personal experience of a large manor house.

Most of the buildings can be touched, but our height will only allow us to explore the lower parts of the buildings. Information that is above our height and out of reach is hard to feel through touch. Going around a building gives information about its size. Getting to know the building indoors gives an experience of its extent, location and the size of the rooms, echo, materials, objects and other details. The following example is of a guided tour of an old church (Lahtinen, 2000):

- *"Our bus arrived at the old church yard. When we got out of the bus, I started to describe generally, where we had entered. We were in a small car park in a forest. Right at the edge of forest there was a 1 m (3 ft) high fence, which surrounded the church yard. It was made of natural uncut stones. There was one entrance through the fence and after that there were old grave stones. The tombstones of the graves were grey, almost covered with grass.*

- *The guide was waiting for us by the church door. There were two entrances to the church. One of them was modern with wheelchair access. The other one was a solid old oak door with a big, round iron ring handle. After description I started to guide the person with visual impairment to the old door and uneven stairs. The church guide called us and asked us to use the modern door. However, we entered through the old door. Just climbing up the stairs with steps in different height levels gave us an experience of old fashioned times. The person with visual impairment opened the door by himself and experienced opening a heavy wooden door. The door opened reluctantly and slowly. At the same time he experienced the old wooden material of the church door..."*

When the describer is preparing a description about people and scenery there are various things to reflect upon:

Who is there? How old? What does he/she do? Where is the person?
- A six-year-old boy is making a bark boat by the lake.

A specification of his actions and description of the boy:
- The boy is sitting on a wooden, grey floating dock. He is wearing knee length blue trousers. He is tanned all over. The boy has blond, short, curly hair showing under a dark cap.

What is there around the boy?
- Around the boy on both sides of the floating dock there are tall reeds in the lake.

What is there in the background of the boy?
- Behind the boy there is large lake scenery without shore.

5.4 Description of a hotel room and accommodation

Description of a hotel or other accommodation relates to travelling. When entering to a hotel you describe the reception desk and give an overview of the room locations (meeting room, ball room, breakfast room, lift). Some people want to get to know their hotel room by themselves, whereas others wish a more precise description. Outside the door of the hotel room the description includes for instance

- landmarks in order to find and leave the room,
- recognition of the room: location of room number, rubber band or other agreed symbol around the door handle,
- relationship of the door to the route and emergency exit and
- how to open and lock the door.

The visually impaired person may orientate to the room by him/herself by walking around it. They may explore the place; directions can be pointed out to him/her by hand to hand contact or spoken verbally. You may walk around the room together and describe at the same time. The overall picture, shape and placement of furniture are given. The general impression of the room is described (lightness/darkness, tidiness) while the description progresses logically. Of a hotel room you describe for instance:

- cloth rack, place for luggage, wardrobe and cupboards, light switches,
- pieces of furniture,
- angles, narrow and dangerous places,
- windows (Are the curtains drawn? Can people see through the window into the room?), position of the ventilation window and how to open it,
- location of balcony, radiator, thermostat and ironing board,
- telephone, number to reception, television, radio and remote controls,
- power outlets, alarm buttons,
- minibar, contents, price list and

- other general things: dust bin, information folder, welcome note.

Of the bathroom you describe

- pieces of furniture, glasses, soap and shampoo,
- toilet paper, how to flush the toilet (if different),
- placement of towels and hair dryer and
- other necessary objects: plug socket, dust bin, how the shower works, floor wipe.

5.5 Description of menu and buffet

When eating out reading menus is part of ordering. Description of a menu may begin by a general description where you find out about starters, main courses and desserts, combined menus available and drinks. The general description includes saying the prices of different food. When you order through a Pizza Service, the description may start from the courses available:

- "From the take away Pizza Service you can order pizza, kebab, steaks, cutlets, salads and drinks. There are 29 different pizzas. You can choose each pizza in normal or family size or as deep pan pizza. The prices of normal pizza vary from 6,90 to 8,70 euros, a family pizza will cost from 12,00 to 14,90 euros and a deep pan pizza 11,30 to 13,00 euros.

- The pizza toppings on offer are; bolognese, which includes minced meat. Frutti including tuna, shrimps and mussels... There are bread, rice and iskander-kebabs. Prices are 5,90 to 8,00 euros. Bread kebab includes kebab meat and salad, rice kebab includes... Cutlets are wiener-, hawaii-, oscar- and swiss schnitzels. Prices vary from 9,90 to 10,90 euros. The wiener schnitzel includes..."

Next time the receiver will vaguely know what there is available. Usually the situation progresses interactively, i.e. the person with visual impairment asks about courses that interest him/her. During the description you tell about possible special offers (price), means of payment and provide other service info.

You can describe a buffet while standing a bit further away or when queuing. On a cruise and during Christmas period there is a wide selection. The describer starts with how many buffet tables there are and which selections are available. The following example is about describing a traditional Finnish pre-Christmas buffet:

- *"There are three buffet tables. There is bread on a side table to the right: a dark Christmas loaf and two different baguettes, dark and light. Beside the bread plates there are butter and spread boxes. On the table in front there are cold fish slices and on the other side of the table cold meat slices. You can walk around the table. Behind the table there is main course buffet. There are boiled, peeled potatoes, carrot and rutabaga casseroles, readily sliced ham and turkey and brown sauce. At the end of the table there are two different mustards and cranberry mush."*

When choosing the courses you can describe the assortments on the tables in more detail. At this stage it is advisable to use a restaurant menu. When coming closer to the starter buffet table the description may be:

- *"In the beginning of the table there are utensils. Plates are on the edge of the table. Behind there are knives on the left and forks on the right. First there are fish courses and on the other side of the table meat courses. The first fish courses are pepper herring, onion herring and marinated herring in pieces. Next is pickled herring, on which there is sliced egg. Then there are thin pieces of salted salmon fillet and smoked salmon fillet. There are no visible bones. After that there is charcoal grilled vendace, which are about the size of your little finger. After that there are peeled shrimps in a bowl and in another bowl there are mussels in their shells. Now we turn to the meat dishes. First there is..."*

A more precise and detailed description includes naming different ingredients:

- *"In tomato-cucumber salad there are alternately thin slices of red tomatoes and fresh cucumber. Above them there is crushed egg with dill."*

The person may take the food him/herself or the food is taken together with the help of leading hand. The describer may fill the plate in accordance with the visually impaired person's instructions or he/she may ask the waiter to serve the meal ready onto his/her plate. Description of courses is closely connected to expression of amounts and description of shapes and sizes. Some people want to know, if the tomato is sliced or chopped, if the onion is chopped or in rings or if the potatoes are peeled, whole or mashed.

There are different ways of describing how much food there is. The receiver may describe verbally or by drawing on his/her own plate, how much of the plate is covered by the portion. The amount can be proportioned to the size of the plate (half a plate, quarter a plate). The amount can also be compared to a familiar target; potatoes are the size of the top of a thumb or egg sized, a teaspoon or tablespoon of red raspberry jam. When the meal is on a tray, you describe the utensils on that, starting from either the right or left hand edge. A clockwise-system is often used to describe a portion (chapter 8).

5.6 Description of arts

A culture expressed in images forms a part of the visual environment. An ideology of accessibility to the arts has been based on visually and dual sensory impaired peoples´ experiences. These provide guidelines describing works of art. Guidelines of description in museums have been collected among others from materials of Finnish National Gallery (Green, 2000) and by people with visual impairment or deafblindness. Honkanen & Vartio (1998) have succeeded in collecting information from those who were born blind about their visual images of the world. Their book enunciates relevant issues on a personal level to be focused on in descriptions by people who are born blind. Visiting an art exhibition (Honkanen & Vartio, 1998, 137):

- *"...a friend explains the colours of the painting and the play of shadow*
- *and light..."*

Because it may not be possible to touch the painting, description provides the possibility to experience the picture contents. The way to describe a painting depends upon the receiver's individual needs. In the following a comment by a person who was born blind (Honkanen & Vartio, 1998, 133):

- *"Any image will become a difficult one if you start explaining it very*
- *meticulously and try to say everything you can see in the picture."*

The artist may have written description of the artwork. A describer or an employee at the exhibition may read that to the receivers. Palmer describes one of his paintings "Old Frinton by the Sea" (picture 8), as follows:

- *"The picture is illustrating a scene from a seaside town´s past in the 1930´s.*
- *The title of this picture is "Old Frinton by the Sea", and was created using*
- *oil crayons in 2007. The picture is a little smaller than A4 size paper.*

5 Description in different situations

- *It is a warm summer early evening. You are standing on the grassy bank near the edge of sloping cliffs looking east. The sea is on the horizon to the right. As you cast your eyes over the cliff top towards the rich green grassy bank, you will see little brown bushes scattered around, looking like Scottish heather. There are white and pinkish puffy clouds in the sky to the left, which are reflecting a sunset at the end of the day, creating different colours in the sky of blue, lilac and yellow. As you scan towards the beach on the right, you see the sea lapping the shore, gently breaking between three wooden breakwaters, creating foam and mixing with the sand. The beach is very sandy with some stones scattered around.*

Picture 8. Old Frinton by the Sea

5.6.1 Description of an individual work of art

When describing a work of art, one suggestion would be first to describe the environment where the art form is being displayed. Begin by mentioning the location of the artwork and name the target. The work will be perceived in the space, when the description includes information on how it relates to the public (direction, the person's distance from the work), placement of the work (on the wall, on the floor, on a table, on a pillar), is it vertical or horizontal and is there a spot light on the target. More precise basic information of the work can be found in information on art works (figure 5) and the presentation folder. The name tag is pointed out and described in relation to the target. The name can be explained letter by letter if necessary. If there are no facts available about the artwork, you tell the subject of the work freely (portrait of a woman, nature landscape).

HELENE SCHJERFBECK

THE CONVALESCENT
Oil painting
3 x 3,5 ft

Figure 5. Facts about the artwork

The work's size, shape, technique (watercolour, oil paint) and material (bronze, cast, iron, marble, wood) are described. Picture frames are described (width, shape, material) and background or platform ("There is a bronze horse on a marble pillar.") A general description of a separate work shows what the work consists of (person, object, abstract work), how it is designed, what there is in the background, colours and atmosphere (someone crying, laughing). Figures and their location are described. The work often also reveals the time of the year. You can tell things about the paintings that are not visible ("There are no fishing boats in the harbour."). If possible, touch it. Of course, you have to have the art gallery's permission to touch objects and wear protective gloves. This is a typical description of a statue (picture 9):

- *"Along the statue-wall, about one metre (3 ft) from the door in a wall niche, there is a one metre (3 ft) tall white cast statue on a 0,5 m (1,5 ft) pedestal. The statue depicts a naked, muscular man whose genitals are covered with a leaf. On the side of his right leg there is a broken log up to his knee. On his shoulders he is carrying a ball with star-like embossed patterns. His face is serious. He has beard, wavy hair and a headband."*
- (Ristimäki, 2008)

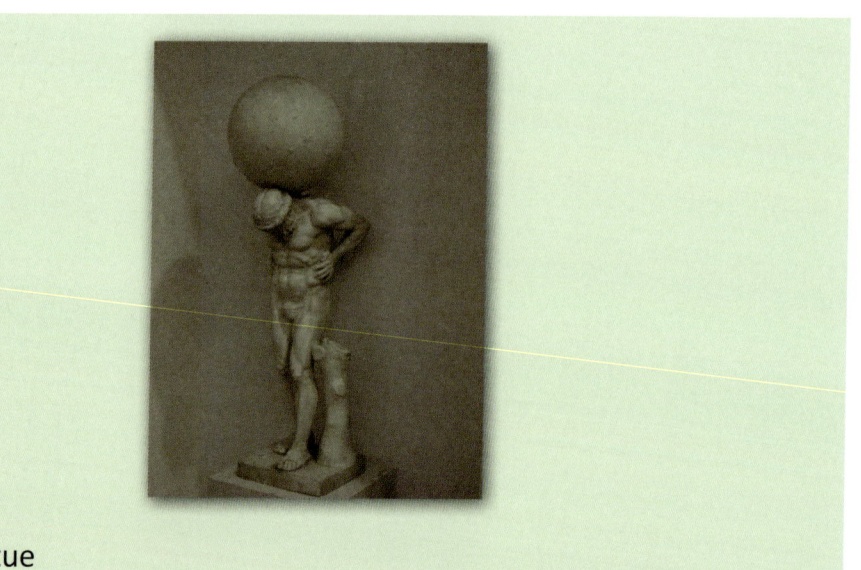

Picture 9. Statue

A detailed description includes a more precise presentation of targets and people (posture, appearance, clothes, size, looks and hair). Describe animals in the artwork, their race, size, colour, looks, posture and other objects connected to them (milk plate, saddle) as well as the atmosphere (picture 10):

- *"In the picture there is a brown wire-haired dachshund named Mökä. The*
- *dog has short legs and long body, viewed from the front up its waist. It*
- *is a side angle view. In front of Mökä there is a striped ice-cream bowl*
- *on a dark green paper carpet. Mökä likes ice-cream, its nose is close to*
- *the bowl when it is licking. On the right hand side of the picture there is*
- *a half-eaten bone."*

Picture 10. Mökä having an ice-cream

5.6.2 Description of a photo

When describing a photo the same principles apply as with a work of art. Identify the photo (a person, a situation, x-ray image, portrait, advert or newspaper photo). You can also clarify the type e.g. snapshot or digital photo. When it is a portrait, you explain, how much of a person can be seen (face, chest, whole body), and how he/she is positioned in relation to the photographer e.g. facing the camera. There is a description of three photos taken in Frans Leijon -meeting room at the Finnish Deafblind Association. Description of the general area gives information about location and how it relates to other photos on the wall. General information tells about the time and how the photos are laid out:

- *"There are three black and white photos on the wall. The photos are in the middle of the wall. The two on the left are close to each other and the one on the right is on its own. They are all rectangular. The photos were taken at the beginning of the 20th century. Mr Frans Leijon is about 40-year-old in each photo in different situations."*

If more precision is required, explain more details using description order. There are no written details available of these photos. Frans Leijon is on a tandem in one photo (picture 11), which is 40 x 28 cm (1,3 x 0,9 ft). It can be described as follows:

- *"In the photo on the left are a young man and a woman. They are sitting outside on a tandem looking directly at the camera covering the front of the picture with their bicycle. She is in front and he is behind. They have been photographed from the front so, that they are sitting on the bicycle with their left side towards us.*

  Because the photo has been shot quite close, only parts of the walls and old-fashioned windows can be seen in the buildings behind them. There is a wooden shed or hut with a pitched roof and wooden fence in the background. Behind the fence there is a part of the neighbours' wooden

- *one-storey house, in the upper left corner there is the gable of the house*
- *and in the upper right hand corner the side of the house with a window.*
- *White curtains are hanging in the window. The shed in front of which*
- *they pose is between the neighbouring houses. The building on the left*
- *is vertically boarded and the one on the right horizontally. There is lawn,*
- *bushes and an over one meter (3 ft) tall tree plant in front. Under the*
- *wheels there is a gravel path without any grass."*

Picture 11. Frans Leijon and a woman on a tandem

For precision add more details. This can be done as a dialogue, where the receiver asks more about the clothes and objects:

- *"The tandem seems to be an adult bike. It has one wheel in front and two*
- *at the back. There are handle bars and pedals both in front and back, but*
- *only the person sitting in front can steer. From the front it looks like an*
- *ordinary bicycle. The frame is metal all over, the mudguards and handle*
- *bar are shiny metal. The frame is painted. The two wheels at the back are*
- *side by side and are connected at the back like a milk cart.*
-
- *The woman sitting in front is wearing a white knee-length dress. She has*
- *a scarf on her head, which is tied under her chin. She looks serious. The*
- *dress has a bell shape. She is wearing black stockings and leather ankle*
- *boots. Both of her feet are on the pedals and her hands are on the handle*
- *bars. The man behind her is clearly bigger than her. He is wearing a dark*

- *suit, under which he has a shirt with a butterfly. However, the suit does not seem to be the Sunday best, but for everyday use. He is wearing leather boots and a wide brim hat. He has a thick, dark moustache. He is focused. His hands are on the rear handle bar of the bicycle and his feet are on the pedals as if he is ready to move off."*

In an individual and a group picture the photos are named by their basic characteristics (individual photo, passport sized photo or class photo). Describe number of people (picture 12) as well as where they are (in two rows, those in front are sitting and those behind standing). You can specify if the people are adults (men, women) or children (girl, boy). ("In the front row from the left there are four women with two men sitting down. One man has a two-year-old boy on his knees."), their age ("A teenager and older woman, around 15 and 80 years of age.") and where they are in relation to the photographer ("Both are looking at the camera, their upper body is visible."). In addition, you can describe their facial expressions ("Both look serious."), what they are doing ("They are probably sitting on chairs."), how they look ("He has a moustache and her hair has been plaited into a tight bun on her head."), the clothes they are wearing and quality of photo ("The photo is unclear.").

Picture 12. Group photo

5.6.3 Description of theatre and music performances

For a theatre performance begin with the stage (furniture, lights), actors' clothes, mimes and gestures. There are many ways of describing different themes, for instance an empty stage and a love theme can be described by using different tones. (Pehrson, 2000) By getting acquainted with the setup and wardrobe of the theatre in advance, you can gather relevant information. Then the description is connected with e.g. exploring the theatrical props. In a music performance describe the performers (band, symphony orchestra, jazz club), instruments and stage.

During a performance you can speak into a microphone, sign, whisper near the other person's ear or use touch messages. Primarily an audio description is used during silences when there is no dialogue. The person with visual impairment can listen to a verbal explanation of events about the scene through headphones.

5.6.4 Description of films

Various facts combine in films. The basic idea is to describe in proper time the actors, operational setting and in terms of plot important clues. This may also include the way the film has been made, presentation of director, interview of screenwriter and voice samples of the actors. Texts at the beginning and end of the film are read.

Chose concepts to describe that match the film's atmosphere and era. You may not have time to explain if specific vocabulary like bandana, while the film is on. In cinema and theatre performances the events advance fast, so that it is important to have seen a performance beforehand and made a description. Focus on relevant information in terms of the plot.

When it comes to a film, the space and stage of the event (setup, props), actors (appearance, wardrobe) and their actions as well as the atmosphere are described. You can say whether there is a general, whole, half, close or special close up picture. Since you are not describing over lines, the time available is often short, so you need to be concise. It is advisable to decide beforehand how to describe people's actions (jumping, bouncing). You only describe what you see, do not anticipate future events. Explain sound sources and personal information related to them e.g. who does what (Turunen, 2008).

In a film age, appearance, environment and changes in environment or setting (indoors/outdoors, city/countryside, road/highway) are described as well as events (a car is on a forest road). Flashbacks, fantasies or memories used in a film are challenging. Try to name them. (Honkanen & Vartio, 1998)

If the film is on a DVD, it can be stopped in order to describe events, places and people. When reading a text aloud you have to embody the different characters in various ways. Name the actors when a new scene starts. While the description is going on, distinguish between the characters by changing your tone of voice or using different signs. Some TV films and DVD´s now have both subtitles and audio description available.

Here is an example of a short television interview. The describer has studied the material beforehand. Before the programme starts, the person with deafblindness is told facts relating to the film and given the names of people as well as ways of communication. This helps the description during the film. Contexts and frames are created at the beginning. Here is an example of the beginning of an interview (Lahtinen, 2000):

- "There is an interview of Sampola's signing choir on the video film. Two of the choir members are interviewed. First they interview AA. She is a person with deafblindness and uses tactile signed language. The other interviewee is BB who has established the choir and is a sign language interpreter. At the end there is brief signed choir performance, the song is by ..."

Exercises and reflections

Description of person
1. If you cannot see your discussion partner, what would you like to have described about him or her?

2. Write a description of yourself on a piece of paper.

Description of space and scenery
3. Describe the space where you are and the scenery you see.

4. Make an audio description of your home street, living room and scenery seen from your window.

5. What kind of description of your hotel room would you prefer to receive? Why?

Description of target
6. Explain to a person with visual impairment the following expressions: aerial landscape art, interior artwork and canvas art.

7. How would you describe your money (notes and coins)?

8. In which shapes can pineapples, tomatoes, carrots and potatoes exist?

A described drawing
9. Draw the assortment on the table by following these instructions:

"You are sitting at a table. There is a plate in front of you. The fork is on the left of the plate and the knife is on the right. A glass is behind the plate at 1 o'clock. A bowl with whole potatoes is at 2 o'clock. Butter is placed between the potatoes and the glass. There is a bread basket with slices of rye bread at 12 o'clock behind the plate and the glass. A frying pan with sauce is behind the fork at 10 o'clock. There is a water jug behind the frying pan at 11 o'clock."

6 Description of colours, details and special situations

6.1 Description of colours

Colours are often described to the visually impaired, because they are not usually tactile. Colours are everywhere, connected with everyday activities telling us about the environment and objects. The colour of fruit or meat demonstrates physical condition; raw, ripe, well-done or out-of-date. Seeing colours is a complex series of functions and the perception of colours is a product of our brain's interpretation. The brain will not change its interpretation of the colour of the target despite different lighting conditions. The correspondence of a verbal description of colours of a target is ambiguous, since a verbal definition of colours includes individual experiences and impressions.

Colours themselves do not include a message. The meaning comes from different contexts. For instance, orange is used for safety purposes and packing materials, in some countries it is related to postal services. Colour combinations used in certain contexts make us think they belong together. Specific warning lights are used on emergency vehicles, for instance a rotating blue light siren is usually placed on the roof of ambulances, fire engines and police cars. Emergency vehicles also have their own specific colouring; yellow or orange with patterns (UK) for ambulance, red for fire engine and usually white or silver (UK) for police car. It is easy to repeat mental images connected with colour, even if you haven't seen them yourself (black is the colour of death, white is a symbol of innocence and peace). (i.e. Honkanen & Vartio, 1998; Huttunen, 2005) If a visually impaired person wishes to receive more precise information on colours, extend properties of colour like tones, darkness, purity and warmth/coolness during description.

Dark colours appear heavier than light ones; similarly low sounds may give a sensation of darkness in comparison to high sounds giving a sensation of lightness. In our mind colours can be connected with shapes, numbers, letters, sounds, pitch or singing voices. A congenitally blind person is able to identify colours through verbal expressions. Certain colours are recognized also by some political parties, sports clubs and other similar groups. They are a part of cultural, national or governmental community, which has its own colour symbols (flags, coats of arms). According to Huttunen (2005), members of the imperial family of China were the only ones allowed to wear the colour yellow. In Egypt gold was thought to be the flesh and blood of the Sun God. Red has been considered supernatural, magic and a returning life force. In Rome only the Emperor could wear a purple. Blue has represented protection of gods and has been used in sacred worship ceremonies. Black is experienced as dignified and festive, whereas white represents hope and emancipation from earthly sins.

6.1.1 Basic colours experienced by people with visual impairment

Honkanen & Vartio (1998) interviewed nine persons with congenital blindness and one with acquired blindness on how they experience colours among others. The interviewees related to colours in different ways, some of them were able to analyse them in detail. Two of the interviewees stated, that it is difficult for a sighted person to describe colours. According to the interviewees, when describing colours, it is useful to explain what they bring to your mind and what they are generally associated with.

The interviewees considered yellow a slightly suspicious colour, too garish, and that is rarely used for clothing. In the answers yellow was connected to the sun, orange, lemon, marigold, chrysanthemum and mustard. Red was connected with feelings. It was connected with warmth (fire and candle), positivity, passion, softness, sensitivity, love, joy, fear and power. They related red in our world to blood, red bilberry, strawberry, apple and the red traffic light. Adjectives such as blood red or bilberry red were helpful. Socialism and Christmas were connected with the red symbols.

In almost all answers, blue evoked associations of water or sky. For the Finnish people blue has a specific symbolic value. Two interviewees mentioned the Blue Cross Flag and one mentioned the Republic of Finland. Blue brought an image of environment or space. Flowers also appeared in statements (pansy, cornflower); in addition the interviewees mentioned sapphire, spectrolite and a blue study-guide (the blue book). Blue is thought to be a cool and cold colour but it is also considered to be calming and positive. Green was connected with nature, specifically forest or nature in general. They related to green positiveness. However, on an emotional level it was also connected with envy and fear. On symbolic level green was connected with a political ideology (The Green Party). The colour evoked a conflict of emotions; calming, beautiful and scary.

Black and white was experienced as two extremities of the same colour. They mentioned the symbolic meaning of the colour. On emotional level black referred to sorrow, dignity and seriousness. It was a colour of power and strength, and had also a positive characteristic. Black was experienced also positively as a symbol of growth (black soil). Also black piano keys were mentioned. Usage of black colour in clothes and the property of black to absorb warmth were listed. White evoked the most elaborate imagery, including snow, sheet, lily, daisy, cloud, salt, sugar, bark and opal. It was considered symbolic or pure.

Orange was less familiar to most interviewees. They knew it is a mixture of red and yellow. Only orange (fruit), sun and scavenger overalls were mentioned as orange targets. Orange was often considered a garish colour. The interviewees knew, that purple comes from red and blue, but there were few personal experiences or associations related to that colour. Mental images of brown varied. Some experienced it as a negative, dirty colour. For others brown was the colour of nature; peaceful and positive. Some appreciated its usefulness. Most often brown was connected with nature (tree trunk, animal, burnt grass, sand) or groceries (nut, coffee, chocolate).

6.1.2 The meaning of colours

Traffic lights guide with colours, shapes and texts. Colours that are used are yellow, blue, green, red, grey, brown and orange. For instance at traffic lights red indicates stop and green allows to go, usually they are even connected with sounds. Yellow/amber tells that the light is changing into green or red. "Stop" and "Slow - Children" warning signs can be described as follows:

- *"A "stop" sign has eight angles and a red field colour. The letters of STOP and borders are white.*

- *Slow – children road sign (UK) has a triangle shape. The borders of the sign are red and the field is white. The silhouette of two running children is black."*

When moving around with a visually impaired person, you can describe general road signs that can also be found on a surface of the road:

- *"The middle line is a broken white line. The continuous line between the lanes must not be crossed. A zebra crossing is indicated with longitudinal stripes across the road. Sometimes different paving materials are used to indicate a zebra crossing. The indication can be made more effective, by adding a sound signal or construction causing vibration, speed bumps."*

During a church year they use alternately five liturgical colours, which are symbolically connected to respective Bible text at that time (colour of the altar cloth, colour of the priest's clothes). White illustrates e.g. brightness, purity and joy, and it also symbolizes the God and Christ. White is used in Advent, during Christmas time apart from Boxing Day, Easter and Midsummer. Green illustrates for instance growth, hope, life force and eternal life and is used from Epiphany until Lent and almost all church holidays after Pentecost. Red is used as a colour of fire and blood, confession and manifesting of Holy Spirit and Christ for instance on Boxing Day, Pentecost, All Saints' Day and Martyr's

Day. Violet illustrates for instance contrition, expectation and preparation on second, third and fourth Advent Sunday, during Lent before Good Friday and during Holy Week. Black is the colour of sorrow, grief, evanescence and death. It is used on Good Friday and often at funerals. (www.evl.fi/liturgisetvarit)

In our culture colours are often connected to the gender of a child. Girls are dressed in sweet pink and boys in cooler light blue. Also in the language of flowers, colours have a symbolic meaning; for instance red means love, white innocence and friendship, yellow passionate love and green peacefulness. Colours are also related to jewels. A red jewel is ruby, deep green emerald and light blue aquamarine. Colours and shapes also form figurenotes-method, where colours correspond to note names, for instance C is red, F blue and H green. Instruments are marked and coloured similarly.

Interesting, illustrating and explaining expressions are connected to colours. How do you explain those in words?

- saffron-yellow: The most expensive spice, saffron, dyed fabric golden-yellow.
- purple-red: The colour was made of an excretion of shellfish gland. First the fabric turned to yellow; later fresh air and sun changed it into purple-red.
- blue-blooded: Members of social upper class avoided tan, so that through their light skin you could see their blood vessels, where the blood seemed blue.
- poison green: The colour was made by using arsenic, which killed people.

6.2 Describing appearances

Various properties of an object are described. These may be height, size, form, amount, distance, length and depth. In addition to a verbal description you can use social-haptic communication. The description will then be made onto and with the help of body, which makes the appearance more precise. (Lahtinen, 2008a)

Expressing height
Height can be described verbally or shown on the body of the describer or the receiver. The object's height level, such as the height where an object is placed (shelf level) is expressed in relation to the receiver's body parts. These are for instance expressions using knee-, hip-, chest-, shoulder- or head-level ("Milk cartons are on your right shoulder level on the shelf."). Height can be compared to familiar things and activities (height of a coat rack, door handle, close to the ceiling, above the window) or to an earlier experience ("The birch is as high as last year´s Christmas tree.").

Expressing size
A size can be compared to a familiar object (plate, egg, postcard) or to an environmental element ("The back yard is as big as a football field."). When describing an object or a picture in a specific format, this can be illustrated by applying the standard three paper sizes i.e. A3, A4 or A5 (figure 6). For example:

- "Within the first rectangular frame there is an A4-size picture placed
- vertically (portrait format). Within the second vertical rectangular frame
- there are two A3-size pictures placed horizontally (landscape format)
- one positioned above the other. Within the third vertical rectangular
- frame there are four A5-size pictures, two side-by-sides on the top and,
- two side-by-sides on the bottom line, symmetrically under the upper line
- (portrait format)."

Figure 6. Different sizes of pictures

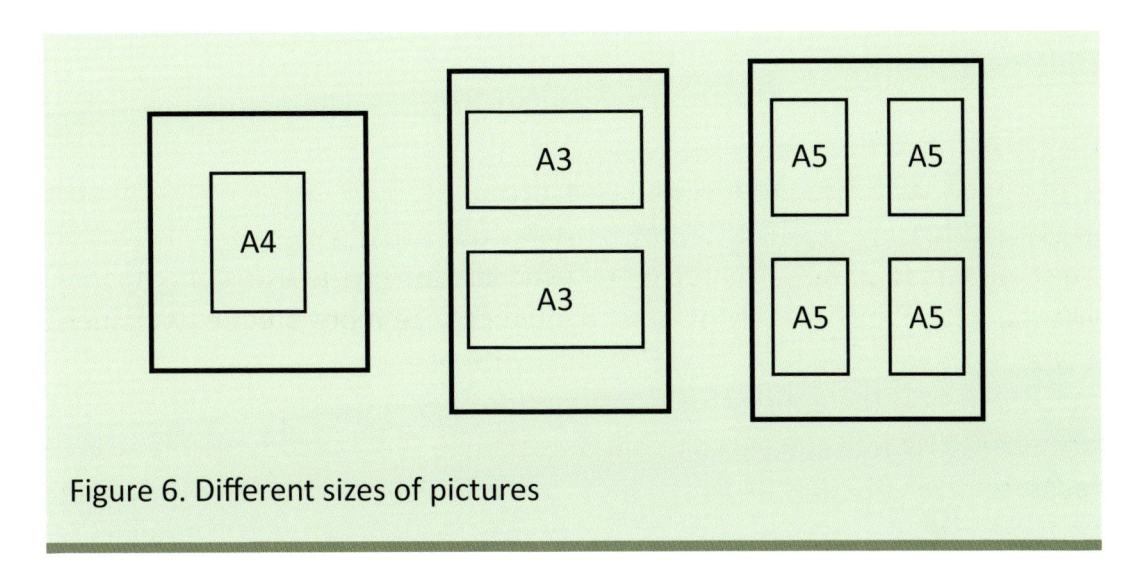

The object sizes can be compared to the objects familiar to the person; using the same length as the white cane or the size of a watch. In order to receive the most precise experience of the size of an object, one has to feel it if possible (thickness of a tree by feeling with both hands). If a target cannot be felt by hand, it can be described using hands on movements. Familiar measures of the body can be used in comparison, such as the thickness of a finger or the thigh. In addition, the size can be shown onto the body or told with body-related expressions (fathom, cubit, span). There are other standardized measurements for instance in terms of the sizes of the paintings in width and height (3 x 3,5 ft) and shelves in width, height and depth (W 1,2 x H 1,7 x D 2,1 ft). In addition there are different sizing systems for clothes for example hooded top sizes XS-XXL, bra sizes A, B and C and shoes sizes 35-46.

Expressing shape
Basic forms of the objects are square, triangle, circle, pile and cross (Frutiger, 1998). In addition, the familiar straight, rectangular and star shapes are used in description. When it comes to the description of clothes, the stripes, checks, decorations and other details can be drawn directly onto the cloth or body authentically. The shape of a target can be compared with a capital letter. In this case the receiver must be familiar with the shape of the visual letter. The shape of a crossing can be for instance L, X, T or Y. The letter can be explained aloud, signed or drawn onto the hand, back, surface of a table or a wall.

Expressing amount

Numbers can be expressed as estimated or precise, such as the number of people in the room ("There are six people sitting at the table."). When there is a lot of people, the amount is usually estimated ("There are about 50 people in the auditorium. The auditorium is totally full."). Estimations will not tell an exact amount neither do they give exact information on the size of the location. With adverbs (much, plenty of, little, a little) the description often gives some guidelines. The expression "much" includes comparison and experience. When describing food there are often expressions of amount included. The amount of groceries is often compared to measures (table spoon, scoop, coffee cup) or measurements (4 l, 198 lbs).

Expressing distance and length

A distance between two points can be described in many ways. The distance can be estimated by the eye in centimetres, metres or kilometres ("The length of the runway is about 300 metres."). The distance can be measured using bodily terms by steps ("The chair is three steps away."). The distance can be expressed in consumed time ("We'll be there in five minutes."). When describing the length of a journey you can attach it to a previous experience ("The swimming pool is as far as the post office."). Lengths can be measured by hand ("The flat panel TV has a palm-wide stand.") or foot ("The gymnastic bench is as wide as foot."). The length of the target is shown directly on the arm or hand. It is easier to perceive the length, when the description of it starts from a finger towards the arm.

Expressing depth

Depth can be described by comparing it to parts of the body ("The water is knee high.") or using the metric system ("The water is 90 cm deep."). The depth can be shown on one's own or the other's body, when the depth is related to the person's height. You can test depth with an object, for instance test the depth of a ditch using the white cane.

6.3 Description of advertisements

In adverts products are presented with pictures and words. A mere picture does not always show all qualities or explain the product precisely enough. The picture is supplemented with an advert text, where some of the basic qualities of the product are explained. The advert text uses basic elements of describing an object (chapter 6.2).

Advert texts describing clothes provide additional facts on the product. Leg lengths in trousers can be expressed precisely ("Leg lengths in men's jeans are 30", 32" and 34"."). Often a speciality or detail included in clothes is mentioned (zip-off trousers, two-way zipper, machine washable, removable hood, leather sock line). Colour expressions spring 2009 connected to clothes were for instance; beige striped, khaki, pink, camel, natural and rouge.

Household utensils are described primarily according to their function and size. Knives are for instance a chef's knife, kitchen knife (big, small), bread knife and vegetable knife. A coffee machine is connected with adjustable temperature and functions related to usage (non-drip system, filter). Cosmetics are advertised to be waterproof mascara or kiss-lasting (longevity power stick) lipstick. Description of glass holders includes primarily expression of colour impressions (blue turquoise, sand, ultramarine blue, bright, bright mat, apple green). Description of flower pots includes their era, colours and materials (antique look, zinc, black rubber, plastic, pine). Thread characteristics include for instance the weight (50 g/clew) or length (sewing thread 200 m). A fishing net is advertised as follows:

- "A high quality double knot fishing net. Mesh sizes 40, 43, 45, 50 and 55
- mm. Height 180 cm, length 30 m."

Description of pieces of furniture includes naming the material (buffalo leather, faux leather, metal, aluminium, galvanized steel, hardened glass, chrome, oiled hardwood, rubber tree, granite, plastic). There are many different kinds of chairs, such as arm chair, folding chair, stackable chair, deck chair, bar chair, office chair, game seat and footstool. A table is usually described by its size (W 80 x L 150 x H 75 cm). Description of a table and stackable chairs:

- "Width of the table is 80 cm, length is 150 cm and height 75 cm. The stackable chair has a grey, aluminium frame. The chair's black seat and back rest are net lace. The arm rests are teak."

In addition to expression of colours and materials, a description of sofa types includes information on other properties (2-seater, 3-seater divan sofa bed). Measures of a shoe shelf are expressed in addition to width and height also depth (W 69 x H 41 x D 26 cm) Sometimes the depth of a shoe shelf is described as file depth. A cupboard can be described more precisely:

- "The white cupboard has two doors. Behind the full-length left hand side door there is a coat hanger holder. Behind the shorter door to the right there are three shelves and in addition three boxes underneath the door."

There are some expressions of advert texts describing special machines listed as follows:

- display (pixel, size of display), effect (400 W),
- RPM (3 000/min), charge current (12 A),
- capacity (2 car ramps maximum capacity 750 lb, tensile strength of the belt 2 000 kg),
- lifting capacity (the lifting capacity of a jack is 2 tons),
- lifting height (jack's lifting height 140-500 mm),
- torque (tensioning device's torque tension 10-210 Nm),
- amount (riveting tool series contains of 10 mandrels, maximum air pressure 6.3 bar/90 PSI),
- use of air (riveting tool series uses 367 l/min),
- number of springs
  (number of springs in box mattress is 113/square metre).

When the advertised product is a bigger entity, for instance a series, package or set, the description will include different parts of the product:

- *"Children's bucket set consists of a bucket, strainer, shovel and three sand*
- *moulds."*

Also special functions and peripheral equipment related to the product are named (Mp3-reproduction, USB and i-Pod interfaces, extra brush, spare key).

6.4 Description of different situations

In description of special situations and targets the terminology of the appropriate field can be used. In this case the describer and receiver are familiar with the contents. In description of church concepts illustrating church areas and objects are used, such as central aisle, side chapels, pulpit, altar and altar-cloth. If the vocabulary is new, a more familiar concept is given as an alternative, or the word is explained. Command of special terminology becomes relevant in description of different hobbies (physical exercises, games, computer, handicrafts).

Description of maps and ground plan
In order to support verbal description a map can be drawn onto body. Drawing areas are often hand, back or thigh. A hand may form a map of Finland, where Helsinki is placed near the wrist and Ivalo, north of Finland, on the top of middle finger. Other towns can be placed between those. In map description compass points (i.e. north, south, east, west) are used. Draw a room or space onto person's back. Use compass points to describe the ground plan of a house including the number of rooms. Start at the entrance and relate the location of rooms to that. The description progresses coherently ("Opposite the entrance there is coat rack and the hallway opens to the left."), the sizes of rooms may also be compared to each other. (e.g. Collin, Kallio & Tala, 1985)

Description of a route
When you are in a new space and getting acquainted with the environment, the route description may consist of the route from a meeting table to toilet, coat rack or outside door. The route can be described verbally, but it can also be drawn onto the body or with a thick soft pencil onto paper. A description of a route from the chair to the coat rack:

- "The coat rack is on your left. When you stand up, the door is at 9 o'clock.
- Turn left after the door and after few steps on the other side of the corridor
- there is a long coat rack. There is a hat rack on your shoulder level."

Description of physical exercise

Description of physical exercises includes description of sequences of movements, different parts of body and expression of directions. Often also illustrating expressions are used ("Cross your hands on your chest, like in praying position."). It is useful to leave out redundant words we tend to use when describing movements. The ending of a movement must be expressed clearly.

In the beginning of the gym lesson the pupil is guided to the correct starting position by the instructor's leading hand, supported by a verbal description. Equipment is used, such as canes, balls or scarves (in different lengths, weights, colours). It is easier to perceive and learn a movement, when a part of the body stays on the same spot (sitting: stable lower body, upper body moves). To make the performing of the exercise easier, the pupil receives a clear signal of how wide the movement should be. For instance, a ball touches the floor when the pupil's movement is extensive enough. You can give rhythm for the exercise speed by counting; with small children by singing and using nursery rhymes. An example of description of posture exercises (Hokkanen, 2009):

- *"Take a seat. Put your feet onto the floor. Straighten your back. Hold the ball with both hands. Lift the ball above your head. Stretch the ball as high as you can. Put the ball back onto your lap. Lift the ball 10 times.*

- *Same start position. Hold the ball with both hands. Put the ball onto the floor on your right. Lift the ball back onto your lap. Put the ball onto the floor on your left. Lift the ball back onto your lap. Make the movement 10 times."*

Even though mental images help to perceive movement, an experience of movement is needed. In the following example mental images are used in describing movements (Hokkanen, 2009):

- *"Sit down on the floor. Bend your legs a little. Imagine that you are sitting in a boat and take the oars. Start to row.*

- *Row to the shore. Get out of the boat. Pull the boat clear of the water. Go swimming. Make breaststroke movements with your hands.*

- *Go onto the floor on your stomach. Lift your arms out as if they are wings. Lift your legs off the floor. Imagine you are an airplane.*

- *Move with the rhythm of music. Lift your arms to the sides and imagine you are a butterfly. Make the movements as light as possible."*

Description of a book and a poem
An audio book conveys the contents of a book as precisely as possible to the listener. For instance citations and text types (italic, bold, quotation) are described from the text. Explain illustrations, tables and graphs. Explain the graphic layout, shape and deviations of poems before reading the text. In an audio book manual (Colling et al., 1985) there are some principles of explaining a picture into a recording. First the picture is given a brief and concise title, which tells what and from where the picture is ("In the photo there is a man and a woman at a café. The picture is black and white."). Next comes the location of parts of the picture ("He is standing behind the table and she is sitting on a chair.") and the directions are expressed precisely ("He is looking at the camera. She is sitting sideways and looks at him."). In addition, the sizes of the parts are expressed in relation to the photo ("The man and the woman fill almost the whole picture."). In the end a general view is created, which explains the atmosphere.

According to the guidelines for readers of audio books the way to read should be that the receiver him/herself can make an interpretation of the contents. A vivid reading of a book includes proper emphasizing, pausing and natural reading speed. Punctuation is guided for instance full stop and commas appear as small pauses. Other punctuation is read out, for instance ¼ (one quarter), 10 km/t (ten kilometres an hour). Abbreviations are usually read whole, such as Dr. (Doctor) and Mrs (misses). If the abbreviation is in common use, it can also be read as it is (EU, UN). (Äänikirjojen lukuohjeet, 1995)

Description of graphic presentation
Graphs and tables are described using vertical and horizontal axis, scales, number of curves and columns, squares or circles (chapter 4.1). The number of columns and rows are explained in of a table. Then the details will continue coherently. (Collin et al., 1985)

Description of writing space for signing one's name
The writing space for a name can be shown either with the describer's or receiver's finger or a pen. The person will be shown where to start writing and the size of the writing space. In locating the space it is possible to also use a ruler, signature guide or folded paper.

Description related to use a computer
In computer teaching it is possible to give messages onto the body on functions and how they are proceeding. Describing the computer screen is based on visual or verbal information. The hands can feel the keyboard while giving the description at the same time. Bodily touch messages are formed in various ways. They can be based on signs and/or vision, beginnings of words produced with capital letters and abbreviations or agreed messages created for the situation. Bodily messages are produced onto the upper back while the person is sitting. With the verbal description you can draw the computer screen onto the back so, that the upper back is acting as the big computer screen. Even the keyboard can be drawn onto the back. Description of a computer onto the body can be used. One computer instructor for visually impaired persons used bodily messages as follows (Lahtinen, 2008a):

- "When getting to know the places on the keyboard with the help of body, the back forms the keyboard. For instance the key "Esc" button is on the upper left hand corner of the shoulder (touch of place) and "Enter" is on the right hand corner down on the lower back (touch of place). The "Space bar" button is in the middle of the back (long line). A connection to tactile information will be established, if the hands are used at the same time on the keyboard. Those who receive spoken information use a so called "speaking" button, in which case their commands + and - are drawn onto corresponding places of the right shoulder. If there is a letter button included, like in browsing (+, z), it is drawn onto as corresponding *a place as possible. Rows are expressed by drawing a long line in the wished direction.*

Windows desktop and screen are drawn as a square onto the back, where icons are shown by a closed or open side of hand in the actual order horizontally line by line. When an instructor wishes that the student will change a function during the touch, the touch is activated on the back with intensity. For instance moving of mouse on the screen is clarified by moving a finger on the back. When it is at the right place, the touch is activated by change of intensity by pressing the finger harder. By drawing onto the body, information is given for instance on places, orders, directions, shapes, processing functions and changes."

Description of handicrafts

For instance, at a lace exhibition bobbin lace works are described to an interested person. In description the terminology related to bobbin lace will be used. "A candle in the church" (Kortelahti, 1979), a bobbin lace picture (picture 13) can be described as follows:

"The bobbin lace work is made by Mrs Aili Lahtinen and frames by Mr Matias Lahtinen in 1990. The picture has been made with linen bobbin thread nr 70 and white gimp thread. In the lace work, 54 pairs of bobbins and one pair of gimp thread have been used. The bobbin is made on a pillow on top of a pricking with the help of needles. The background is of linen fabric. The size of the picture is vertically 39 cm and horizontally 31 cm. The frame is a 4 cm wide moulding. The lace part is vertically 21 cm and horizontally 15 cm. The upper part of linen fabric is 4 cm, edges 3,5 cm and bottom 6 cm wide.

"A candle in the church" – lace work illustrates a church window, on the windowsill of which there is a roundish candle on the right. The window is filled with details made by using different stitches. Whole stitches and cloth stitches have been used on the upper right hand corner of the window. On the upper left hand corner the cloth stitches form squares. In the middle of the work there is a vault. The left side of it is made by

net stitches and right side by cloth stitches. In the arc under the left arc circles have been made by whole stitches and twisting the thread. They are framed by a stronger, white gimp thread. The third arc is under that and it is made by cloth stitches. The candle is made by cloth stitches and the wick is formed by a leaf stitch. The flame is made by cloth stitches and the surrounding light has been made by whole stitches and twisted thread. The background of the candle has been made with whole stitches.

The lace part is manually fastened onto the linen fabric. First a hem has been made at the edges of the fabric's cut part by crocheting, after which the lace has been fastened with hemstitches. There is a black background under the lace part against which the bobbin work "A candle in the church" made of linen thread stands out. The frame moulding has been painted dark brown and in the middle of it there is a grey stripe. The fabric is covered with a mat glass."

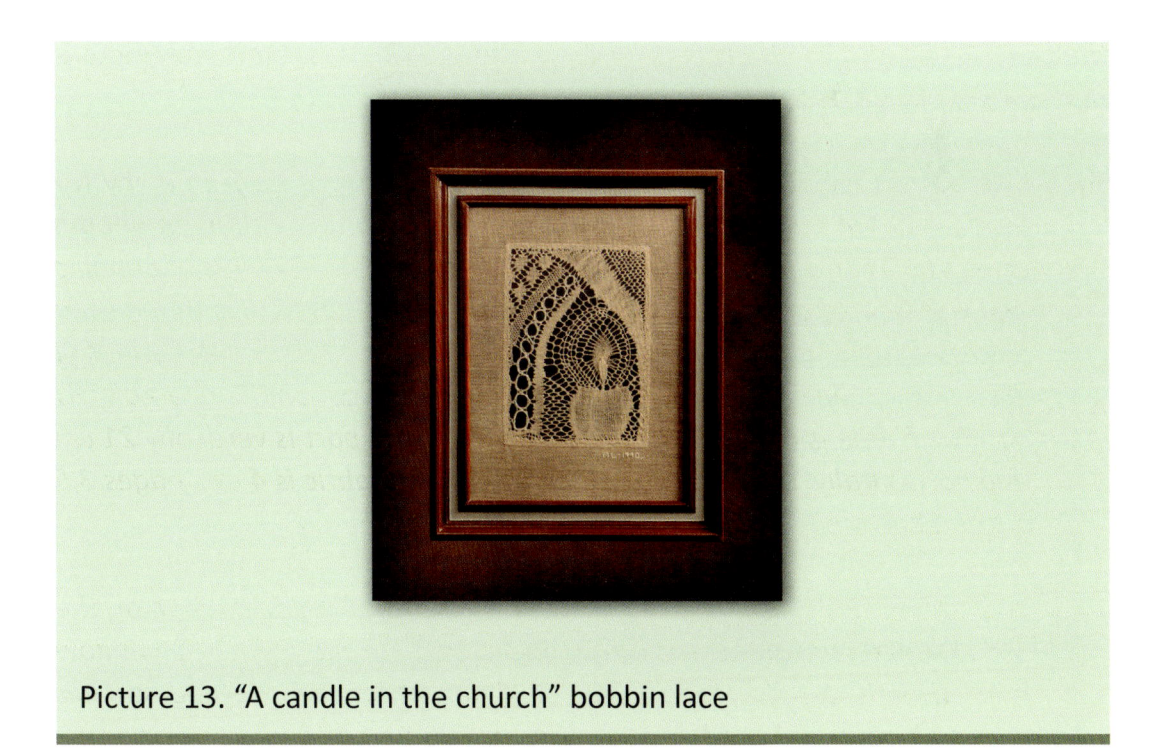

Picture 13. "A candle in the church" bobbin lace

Exercises and reflections

Images of colours

1. Add your images of the colours on the line. Compare your images:

White as _____.   Blue as _____.

Green as _____.   Brown as _____.

Yellow as _____.   Red as _____.

Black as _____.   Grey as _____.

2. Which colour would you connect to the following occupations?
   - nurse, surgeon, police

3. How would you describe the following colours?
   - marine blue, sky blue, electric blue, pitch black, rust-brown, mouse grey

4. Collect the red and green expressions you know.

5. Look around you in a space with a lot of people. How would you describe the general colour of clothes?

6. What are today's fashion colours?

Drawing shapes

7. Pair work; one of you draws the shapes below. Shapes are drawn (blind folded) on palm, back or surface of the table. It is useful to try different methods. The receiver gives feedback on information received either by drawing in the air, on the table surface or paper. Change roles within pairs. Reflect and discuss, which way feels clear and functional.

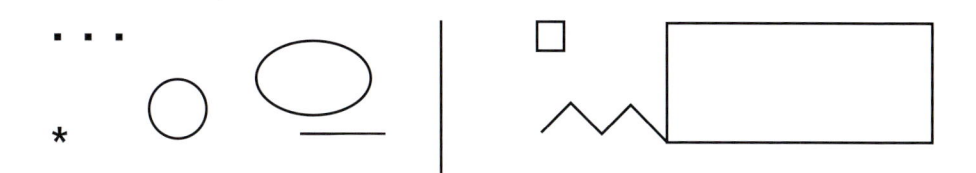

Environmental objects

8. Explore the objects in your environment that can be described with the following shapes: - straight, circle, square, rectangular, oval, cone

Advert texts

9. Collect descriptions of products from magazines.

Description of exercises

10. Describe various exercise movements to another person (blind folded). The receiver does the exercises according to your instructions. Which exercise movements are difficult to express verbally? Which movements are difficult to receive based on verbal instructions only?

7 Describing onto the body

Long verbal descriptions can be avoided by using various bodily expressions. There may be noise and bad lighting in a situation, so you need to concentrate to communicate. In these situations it is quicker to show various things directly onto the body. Haptices are touch-related messages conveying onto the body. Haptices can be used to express behaviour, changes in the environment and events, describe spaces, produce social quick messages and describe competitions and arts. A shared action makes it possible to describe events and objects that are far away and not touchable. Since describing onto the body demands physical closeness, you have to agree on the methods to be used. It is possible to describe diversified information onto different parts of the body (Lahtinen, 2002; 2008a):

- onto the palm and back of the hand; facial expressions, feedback and shapes,
- onto the thigh; competitions, the location and movements of actors either at the theatre or in films,
- onto the back; facial expressions, feedback, orientation in the environment, competitions, shapes, proportions, size, colour, environmental events and landscapes and
- onto the whole body; feedback, movements, moving from one place to another, musical rhythm and hobbies.

Arts can be experienced independently or experiences can be shared with another person. In an **interactional description** experiences are shared by body movements. It is easier to create a mental image out of a three dimensional target than of a mere surface of a painting or photo. In description a touch message onto the body is used independently, as a supplement to verbal information or as a combination of these two methods. Use of combinations shows how well and effectively the methods work, when they support and complement each other. This demands the receiver to really focus. (e.g. Lahtinen, 2005b; Ritala, 2006) The balance between verbal description and the information shared with touch may alter. You can use combinations of other senses. (e.g. Lahtinen, 2001a; 2004)

7.1 Use of hands and objects during description

Exploring an object with your hands allows your own interpretation. A person can explore an object, miniature or raised image independently. In varying lighting conditions the visually impaired rely primarily on touch to get a mental image an object. Touching can add an art experience depending on the way the art work has been created. Mrs Koljonen, a blind sculptor, explains at an interview, that you cannot compare verbal description with the information received through touch (Heikkinen, 2008). Exploring paintings and pictures with hands does not usually give a mental image of the contents. When a person is exploring an object, he/she is active. (Gibson, 1962, 1966; Goldstein, 1989) By exploring actively you get a mental image of a target, its action and movements, space, spatial proportions and different surfaces (Kendon, 1993; Millar, 1997). Residual vision can allow more precise study of an art work.

Exploring an object with your hands during description gives information on various things. By touching you can recognize object's material (metal, plastic, wood), temperature (cold, hot), hardness (hard, soft, flexible), shape (circle, square), size (small, big) and weight (heavy, light). (e.g. McLinden & Graeme, 1999) It also reveals other properties (smooth, multi-dimensional, rough). At the same time the use and function of the object becomes more precise. The use of hypotheses is connected with exploring (teddy bear – Does it have eyes?). A certain smell may relate to an object and it may give out a sound.

Name and give a basic description before exploring, so the receiver knows how to approach the object (fragile, dirty, hot, heavy). This allows independent exploration by:

- leaving out the description of self-evident properties,
- saving both parties' energy,
- transmitting the information to be described quickly,
- giving many facts about the object simultaneously,
- utilizing previous experiences and memories and
- the fact that the received information is personally experienced.

Using an object in description means according to Lahtinen (2008a), that visual information is transmitted through an object and touch. In order to make the description more precise, it is possible to include another object to play the role of the target (a pencil as a baton). The movement or appearance of a target is expressed by an object and movements. For instance during pottery classes the describer may use a piece of clay or at a dance performance a scarf to describe the movements of the dancer's hands and scarf. This creates a more concrete experience of a performance.

7.2 Body and movements during description

Attach pointing to a verbal description in front of the target from different distances at the same time, alternately or in sequence. To point out a target involves showing direction and location, so that the receiver gets information through his/her vision. Pointing is usually done by a finger, palm, whole hand and arm, lower arm or by an object. The leading hand may specify the location of the target and may be changed into a describing hand by drawing the contours of the target in front of it. The hand or hands of the receiver lay softly on the describer's hands. Drawing into the air may be done from various distances. If the receiver wishes to use his/her residual vision to perceive the drawing in more detail, the distance to the target is usually shorter.

At exhibitions and museums there are various statues, which may be out of reach, or cannot be touched or are too large to be explored. **In a mirror description** the receiver explores a posture made by the describer (posture description), movement (distance, action) and facial expressions and gestures. These may also be done onto the receiver's body or together on both people's bodies. Both may also have a posture or role of their own, when they together mirror the target as a whole. The describer must have a capacity to notice the relevant messages of the target and transmit them with his/her own body. (Lahtinen, 2008a)

In movement description the describer's or receiver's own body movements express for instance the target's posture, role, rhythm and the way the movement is made, its duration, extent and pauses. Body movements thus express the location, height, movement and distances of the object. A moving target is described by holistic body movements. Making the movements together will function either as a support to language information or independently. In an action that demands a lot of movements (dance), it is useful to include the receiver's body movements. For instance, a description of a drummer includes a starting position, i.e. the person's posture in the initial contact (the describer places the receiver's hand into the starting position for drumming), contact posture i.e. a change in position connected with exploring the environment (the describer and receiver together form the initial posture for drumming) and action (the drumming). With methods of body movement information is shared on the describer's body (the receiver explores the describer's body and follows the body movements), together on both bodies, and by or onto receiver's body (physical exercises). (Lahtinen, 2001b; 2008a; Lahtinen & Virtanen, 1996)

Body contact in describing a movement can be back-to-back, foot-to-foot, hand-to-foot etc. For instance in relaxation or exercise situations the description of movements may be done either with a part of body, hand, foot or whole body. The use of a leading, describing hand allows the describer and receiver to act in the space. The movement depicts many things at the same time. Sometimes the describing hand acts as the target of description (sea), sometimes it points out directions, but mostly it describes movements.

You need a safe space for the mirror description and movement description to function. There must not be upper, lower or side obstacles nor level changes. The receiver must have time to react to movement. While the receiver is making the body movements, the describer is supporting him/her actively and preventing any collisions. When moving together, the describer can sense the receiver's rhythm and possible difficulties in balance or in making a movement. For instance boxing can be described with movements from hand to hand. The describer and receiver are standing face-to-face and their hand contacts are in dialogue position representing different boxers. The receiver follows the describer's movements. With movements from hand to hand it is possible to describe the actions of two people simultaneously. (Lahtinen, 2008a)

A pantomime can be described by holistic movements. Then the receiver will share the sensation of art merely by receiving touch and movements onto the body. If there is music involved, it will give the rhythm to the action. In a pantomime the bodies or body parts of the describer and receiver participate in creating the movements. They can be received passively or actively. In a passive reception the person feels the movements, whereas in an active reception he/she is involved in the movement. The describer chooses basic movements, postures and action of the characters in a pantomime. When the receiver reacts to those, then produce a new movement. (Lahtinen, 2008a)

Sensation description demands an agreement of the methods used and courage to receive information on the body through experiencing sensations and emotions. Arts can be watched by ceasing to enjoy the atmosphere, the narration of a picture. A drawing, painting and picture are 'stagnated' images that still live in mental images. For instance the atmosphere, colouring, rhythm and size of an art work are telling a story. People seek different experiences; art sensations at an exhibition, excitement at a funfair and nice feeling of togetherness at the theatre. An example of a sensation description is taken from the Tivoli of Copenhagen in 1990's. A person with dual sensory impairment wanted to experience the ghost train. Before entering the train, an agreement was made, that in the dark tactile signs will be used and targets pointed out while the train is moving. In advance it was known, that the scenery will change quickly, and that it will be dark with plenty of different light effects. This was how the first train trip went (Lahtinen, 1995):

The journey started.

- *A ghost (pointing with a hand up to the ceiling).*
- *The ghost is coming closer (pointing out the location of the ghost with a hand).*
- *Running rats (pointing downwards to the locations of rats).*
- *Skeletons (pointing at the skeletons).*

When we came out of the train we reviewed whether the sensations had been as expected. No, they had not! Why do people want to take a ghost train and pay for that three-minute experience? He had expected to scream, frightened and experience horror safely. He shared his wishes and we took the train again. We used the body to describe quick changing situations and ambiences. The second train journey was like this:

- *A ghost. (A ghost is described by hands in strangling shape approaching on the thigh).*
- *The ghost is coming closer. (The strangling hands are approaching the receiver's throat along his arm).*
- *Running rats. (The describer's fingers are running on the receiver's legs upwards biting the leg).*

- Skeletons. (The describer falls down to the receiver's lap playing dead. The describer is sawing the receiver's arm describing the sawn parts of the skeletons.)

The visually impaired person was screaming, laughing, cringing and was engaged in the situation.

Description when moving is related to moving together and guiding. Landmarks are used when moving together (pavement, sand, building). While moving together, targets that need to be recognized along these routes can be expressed verbally, by pointing, with body movements or directly onto the body (lift, door, traffic lights). Description allows better orientation in terms of naming targets, distances, sizes and routes.

Body movements during guiding give information on the environment while moving together. Description related to this includes messages produced by and received onto the body. Body messages give advance information of upcoming action and make targets reachable by hands. Lahtinen (2008a) divides them into different groups depending on the contents of the messages, natural body movements or reactions:

- basic level movements (going around the target),
- emphasized movements (level change),
- agreed guiding signs (narrow passage),
- the target is pointed out with the guiding and leading hand (chair),
- agreed special messages (alarm sign big X) and
- special messages on individual level (the receiver in a wheelchair).

Social quick messages as a part of description are agreed messages produced onto the body; they can be given silently and almost secretly to another person without disturbing the situation. These are for instance messages expressing how the discussion is proceeding (head movements), messages about activities or changes in action (someone left or arrived). The message can be given as a directional touch and expressing the location of the target (kitchen, bathroom). (Lahtinen, 2005a; 2008a)

7.3 Drawing onto the body

Drawing onto the body is an area of description, where the environment is described onto the body, to be recognized through the skin. It may be difficult to describe and perceive description of a target verbally, and then drawing may assist in the perception of the given target. Drawing provides information of the space, objects and relations of events. It supports and complements the receiver's perceptions. It is fast and saves energy. The target is illustrated by drawing with a finger or hand onto the receiver's back, hand or thigh. Then the describer produces with her/his hand the visual shapes of the surroundings, showing people's behaviour, action and arts. Later it is possible to come back to the mental images created by the drawing.

The describer transforms the visual and/or auditory information by drawing it onto the body, which the receiver recognizes, interprets and relates to his/her experiences. For instance, a person who is listening to a lecturer through a loop system can get the presented tables drawn onto his/her back, hand or surface of the table. The lecture hall can be drawn onto the receiver's back as a map, which helps him/her create a touch-based mental map, its shapes, order of objects, directions and routes as well as to locate important areas for orientation (doors, windows, his/her own seat). Social information about people, their reactions and movements are also placed onto the map. (Lahtinen, 2005a)

Drawing can be done onto various surfaces (bag, table, wall) or directly onto an object. When drawing onto the surface of a table, it is useful to have a dark background under your hand. It is easier to pick out what is happening. The receiver can follow the hand movements with his/her residual vision. When sitting side by side usually one hand is used for drawing, whereas both hands can be used when sitting face-to-face. Drawing can be done onto an item to show patterns and colours on cloths and textiles, following the patterns or paintings on an item or picture, or tracking the pattern of frames (tracking description). (Lahtinen, 2008a)

When drawing onto the surface of a table, the receiver's hand or finger can feel the produced movements. When drawing into the palm, the describer can draw with the receiver's finger or his/her own finger, when the receiver's finger is following the drawing finger or using the receiver's index finger as a pen. When drawing into the hand usually the palm is used, sometimes even the back of the hand. It is possible to draw large entities onto the back. Drawing onto the body is either done by one or two hands, depending on the postures and orientation of the bodies.

Description by drawing demands a certain experience of the describer and the receiver. It is important to agree on the principles followed in drawing. Over time and experience it is possible to convey even more complicated and demanding targets through drawing. Drawing is done without hurry, so that the receiver has time to get a mental image of the drawing. It is difficult to perceive abstract figures, if they cannot be connected to something familiar. By drawing it is challenging to describe proportions, perspective and distance. When drawing is used, it is preferable to place things and targets from the receiver's point of view, so that the space will open in front of them. (Lahtinen & Pölönen, 2005)

7.4 Describing hobbies onto the body

It is possible to describe various hobbies onto the body. In the following there are haptices used for describing onto body in relaxation situations, used most often in instructed situations. These are: relaxing, breathing, showing movement, tensing and relaxing muscles, expressing the rhythm of music, closing one's eyes and finishing the session. (Lahtinen, 2008a)

Description of a bowling and an adapted indoor Curling game
When describing games and competitions onto the body, an agreement is made on the ground map of the competition, starting locations, route, goal posts / finishing post and territories of the teams. Also an agreement is made on how to describe the movement of the teams. The walk-haptice is used as a basic movement, which can be changed into different variations of walking (slow, fast, run, stop, fall). If there is a moving item involved, the information on the competition can be given through the movements of the item (ball, disc, javelin).

In various ball games a match between two teams can be described onto the back, thigh or other surface. By describing with two hands, the hands represent different teams. Before the game an agreement is made on messages connected with the match and areas of the playing field. At the beginning of the match the area, rack, distances and direction of items connected with the game are discussed. In bowling, the bowling lane, approach, pins and gutter are drawn onto the back. The side of a hand or fingers move the same direction as the bowling ball (straight forward, to the left or right, into the gutter). Touch information onto the back will show where the ball is heading. Description of the visual progression of the bowling ball in various places of the lane will tell the bowler, how his/her way of throwing influences the progression of the bowling ball. On the basis of this information he/she can adjust his throwing direction if necessary. You can show points, results, speed in which the pins are falling and the standing pins' locations on to the body. In bowling it is possible to use visual special signs, such as strike (X) or spare (/). In a miss the places of remaining pins are described or their numbers are expressed (figure 7).

7 Describing onto the body

Bowling

10 pins in a triangle-shaped battery.

Bowling ball rolls on lane.

Thrower A, Describer B

Adapted indoor curling

The house consists of 3 rings surrounding the button.

The stone is delivered along the sheet.

The curler/thrower is on the other end of the sheet.

Thrower A, Describer B

Figure 7. Basic maps of bowling and adapted Curling drawn onto the back

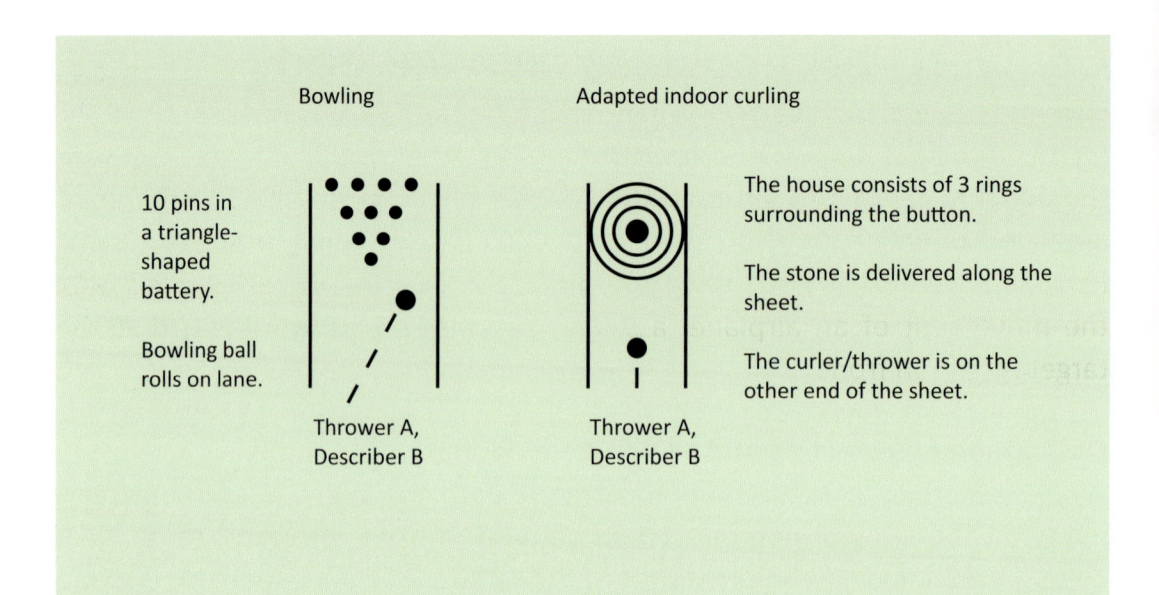

In adapted Curling the travelling of the stone along its path to the target is described. It is drawn onto an agreed area of the back, where the button point and the three surrounding zones are described as circles. The middle point is separated by applying stronger hand pressure. The zones will be shown during the action, so that the player gets information on the place of the stone in relation to the zones. There are some general things in describing these games;

- first you describe the playing field and its shape,
- the player is placed at the end of the lane (by pointing with the two fingers together-haptice),
- you describe the way the ball moves (speed) and its direction with a continuous line,
- you describe where the targets are placed simultaneously with the moving of the ball,
- you describe the change in the target (strike, hit),
- you use social quick messages (feedback, direction) and
- you use agreed special messages (strike, spare).

At an air show the movements of airplanes are described. Often this information changes quickly. When describing a moving airplane there are many simultaneous pieces information described onto the back, for instance the appearance of the airplane to the scenery, flying direction, number of airplanes, their flying paths, speed and height. The following series of pictures illustrates describing by drawing onto the back (picture 14). When describing the movement of an airplane, a single, stronger pressure means, that the target is right in front.

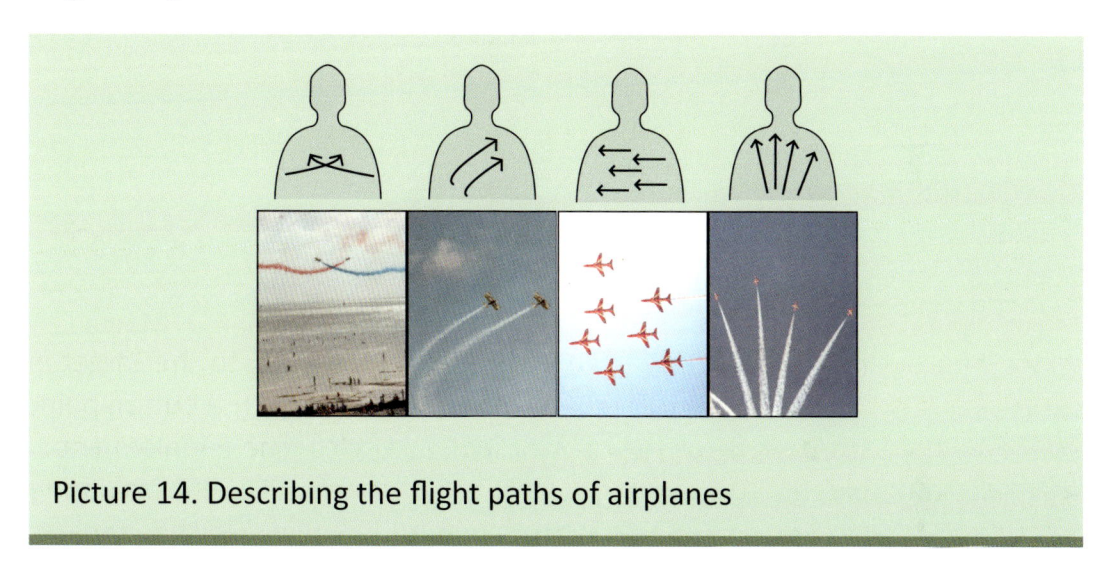

Picture 14. Describing the flight paths of airplanes

When describing dance, the movements are described onto the back with variations of a walk-haptice. They describe how the dancer moves; standing, turning, feet movements, speed and locations. Figure 8 expresses how music and Flamenco-dance are described by touch onto different parts of the body. In the example the receiving parts of the body are shoulder (instruments when the music is proceeding); upper arm (rhythm, melody, level of voice, height) and upper back (the scenery opening in front of the spectator, rhythm, melody). When a dancer is moving on the stage, the teasing approach of a dancer etc. will be brought by varying the distance between the bodies of the describer and receiver.

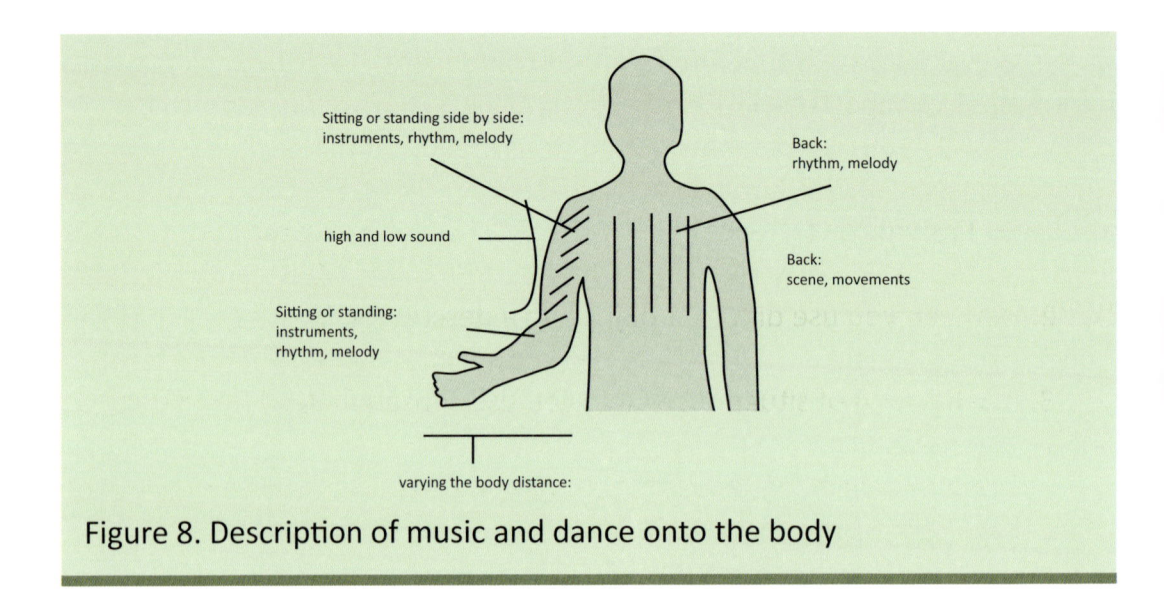

Figure 8. Description of music and dance onto the body

Music can be described onto the body with the help of touch (i.e. Mactavish, 2001). Changes in touch mediate different experience and elements of music. Three levels of expressing music onto the body are noted; the instruments, different elements of music and the artistic experience related to music (dance performance). With the sense of touch basic instruments and variables related to playing an instrument, such as rhythm, direction of movement, pressure and pauses are distinguished from the touch. Several variables are related to a typical movement of playing a particular instrument. (Lahtinen, 2008a)

In the Body Story (Lahtinen & Palmer, 2005) a story is shared with another person by agreed touch movements onto the arm or back. The touch messages of the story can be agreed onto different parts of the body ("The hand is an island, the arm is the shore."). The story can be planned or created spontaneously in the situation or told by a third person. The receiver may participate in the body story actively by creating mental images or letting it relax. There may be music in the background. This method is recommended in descriptive situations, where it is difficult for the receiver to listen to spoken language and music at the same time. This method has also been developed further with fairy tales. Then the texts of the book are read and the pictures drawn onto the child's body, for instance onto the back. (Lahtinen, 2007)

Exercises and reflections

Different methods of description

1. Explore mirroring techniques when you describe a statue.

2. How can you use different objects in a description?

3. In what kind of situations would you use sensation description?

4. Draw the changing landscape as a car moves along the road onto the back of the other person.

8 Pointing directions

Pointing directions is another description area. It can be used both singly and in a group. Pointing of directions must be clear for the receiver. The method depends on the receiver's functional vision, extent of the vision field, lighting conditions, distance from and size of the target. Certain situations may limit the use of some methods, for instance if you cannot stand side by side or use other objects to support the pointing of direction. It is even possible to show directions to profoundly blind person. (Lahtinen, 2008a)

Pointing is considered a gesture-related action. Pointing towards the direction of a target can be made with various parts of the body either consciously or unconsciously. Pointing at a target is a conscious action together with spoken language/signing or a silent independent action for instance when starting to shake hands (the guest arrives, shown his location and height of the hand) or if something special happens in that environment (pointing to the source of a sudden loud noise). Directions can be described visually without touch (head movement, glance) and by touch (leading hand) or and by combining and using them simultaneously (Lahtinen, 2008a).

Speaking or signing the direction of the target is expressed from a certain distance. After receiving the information the receiver looks for the target by using his/her residual vision. In spoken language use clear sentences and expressions of targets. For example an unclear expression "Go there." is expressed rather "Go straight ahead and slightly left. You will be by the wall.". Pointing using a pronoun (this, that, there) without a context or information expressing direction is inaccurate. Directions such as on the left, right, in front, behind or above are not always precise either. **A glance or head movement** points out the direction and position of the object. The head movement can be exaggeratingly slow. A finger and hand may follow the gaze as a route is described.

Lights, shadows and contrasts can be used in pointing directions when the space is dark. Light in the environment helps one find direction by pointing at a light in a window, lamps, street lights and outdoor lighting. If a person has a torch, he/she can use it to make it easier to find the object. In the dark a torch is practical as it simultaneously gives additional light for exploration. Shadows (dark tops of trees against the sky) show the direction of a road or route. If the person can see light and shadows or perceive the environment by distinguishing contrasts, it is possible to express directions by following a clear contrast (a stripe on the floor).

Pointing at the target **with a hand or finger** locates the place, shape or movement as well where the target is and other details of an object. The description is produced by different hand forms and change of movements. The hand or hands of the receiver lay gently on the describer's hands. With your leading hand you can describe the amount, speed and intensity of the target. The leading hand also transmits to the receiver the method of exploring and holding the object. When describing shades of colour certain movements, hand shapes and changes in pressure (heavy, light) are used. They give an insight into the artist´s work; brush strokes, shapes, thickness of colours, directions and overlaps. When pointing and using the leading hand it is possible to use elements of sign language (proportion, localisation, size).

Hand to hand movement description is based on natural body movements, pointing and description of shape. When using tactile signing, it is part of the sign language itself. It is not always accurate to point a direction from a certain distance with a hand or finger, but it gives a clue about whether the object is on the left or right. When signing to a person, one has to notice his/her reactions after having pointed a direction. If he/she is seeking the target with his/her gaze, a pause is kept in signing and it is not continued until the eye contact has been re-established. If he/she is a lip-reader, an eye-contact is established before starting to talk. The direction is given from the point of view of the person with visual impairment, when attention is paid to his/her use of vision and body orientation related to the target. For instance, when pointing at shelves and the position of items in a shop, advance information is given of their direction. Even for a non signer, pointing with a hand and finger is a practical way to provide information quickly even for a person with narrow vision field. Together with spoken language this will immediately provide location information.

During the description point at more distant target **with a white cane or another instrument** when pointing with a hand does not give an accurate enough direction. When the cane is used for other purposes than feeling the route, one has to know how to use it safely, so you don't accidentally hit other people or items. Shapes on the ground, objects (shape of flagstone) can be pointed with the help of a white cane. The moon or bright star in the night sky may be found in a wide nature like this. Also smaller and closer items can be pointed at with the cane, such as patterns of a carpet or an item on the floor. The description will be supported by exploring with a cane, when information about the size, shape, length or depth of an object can be received. (Lahtinen, 2008a)

There are other instruments you can use to point out direction during description. The direction is guided through a perceived object (behind the mouse pad) or according to a line to be followed (on the right of the door, edge of the carpet). The gaze can be directed with an object, such as pointing with a pencil or finger the song text or space for signature.

The use of **the clock system** as a support for spoken language, signing or description on the body gives the direction and location of the target. A mental image of the clock face will facilitate determining a direction. When an object falls onto the floor, it is not always possible to hear the direction where and how far it fell. For instance "to the left" can mean anything around the person 7-11 o'clock and "to the right" the area of 1-5 o'clock. The clock system gives a more precise direction to look and it can even give the exact location of an object.

The picture here shows a suggested way of using the clock system. The receiver is in the middle of the clock face as a part of the surrounding space (figure 9). The time is expressed from the orientation of the person's middle body, not from his/her head position (the head position may be changed slightly). Use hours 1-12; 12 o'clock is in front of the person (a nose always points at 12 o'clock), 6 o'clock is behind, 3 is on the right and 9 on the left hand side.

Figure 9. A clock face with a person in the middle

With the clock system, the target, its level and time (a church in the valley at 4 o'clock) or distance (a pencil at 7 o'clock, two steps) can be expressed. In a moving vehicle (car, train) the direction of the target changes quickly. If a visual impaired person wants to see the target, you have to add to or subtract about two hours from the time when describing a direction. Also objects and targets (plate, TV-screen) may form the bottom of a clock face (figure 10).

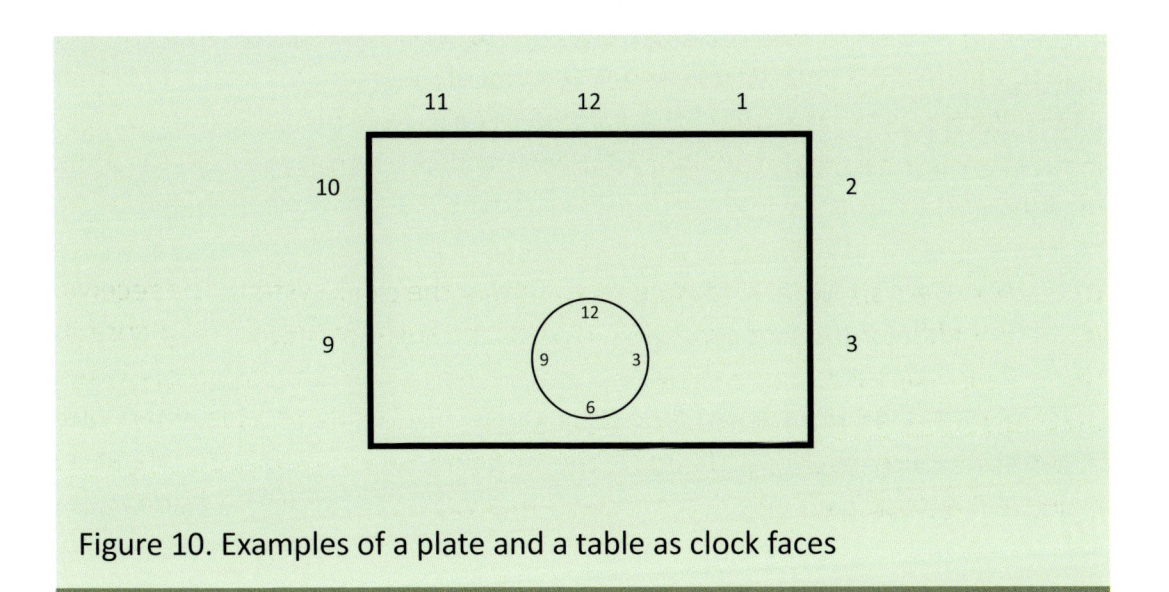

Figure 10. Examples of a plate and a table as clock faces

A clock face may be created onto various parts of the body, such as palm, back (picture 15) or thigh. Then the describer's hand will point in that direction, which makes it unnecessary to express the time separately.

Picture 15. A clock face on a person's back

The use of the clock system gives the receiver the chance to find his way independently. It is easy to use and it saves seeking energy. It can be used in different situations:

- outdoors in order to find surroundings, views, tourist attraction and target
  - The door to the retail store is at 5 o'clock.
  - The water fall is at 8 o'clock.

- in description of space when pointing at the directions of table, chair and door
  - The door is at 7 o'clock.

- in locating an object
  - The coffee cup is on the table at 2 o'clock.

- when seeking a fallen object
  - *The coin is on the floor at 1 o'clock.*

- socially when explaining the location and arrival of an approaching person, so that the visually impaired can prepare by turning towards the approaching person
  - *Mr Smith is approaching from 5 o'clock.*

- in guiding and hobbies
  - *Your bowling ball is rolling towards 11 o'clock.*

- explaining the oven temperature
  - *e.g. 150 °C is to 5 o'clock, 200 °C is 6 o'clock and 250 °C is 7 o'clock*

- explaining where food, beverage and utensils are
    e.g. the table will be formed of expressions of time;
    9 - 10 - 11 - 12 - 1 - 2 - 3 (figure 10).

Compass points are used when describing street directions, illustrating routes or using maps. The cardinal and intercardinal directions can be found on figure 11.

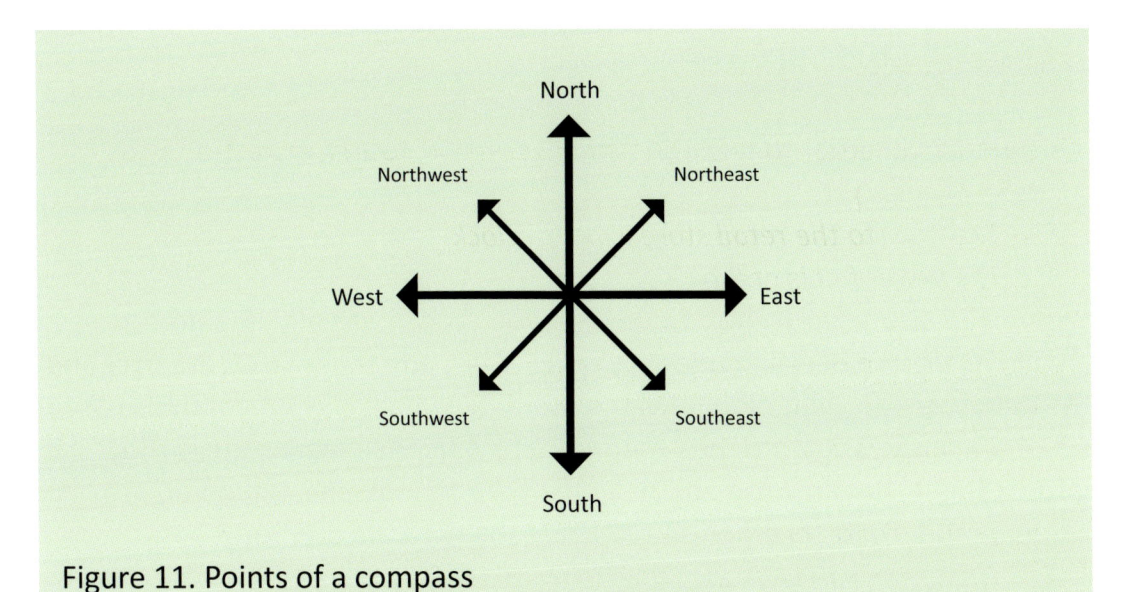

Figure 11. Points of a compass

A seen target can be chosen as a starting point and location for description. In order to find the target the person's **own description of the perceived object and direction of hand movement** are used. Then the visually impaired person explains the target he/she can see in the environment, with this information a new target can be found. This gives the describer an idea of the direction and height he/she sees. (Lahtinen, 2008a) For instance a star in the sky can be found in a situation as if in a picture 16. First the house is perceived and the left edge of its roof. Then the gaze and hand follow upwards until you find the moon. From the moon the gaze moves towards 10 o'clock. You can even support the spoken language by drawing onto the back.

Picture 16. Finding a star in the night sky

Blowing is also used to point out direction. When visually impaired person should focus on a certain target with their eyes, and their hands are occupied, the describer can then blow towards them. Blowing gives lots of information simultaneously; someone has entered you personal space, the airflow can inform about the direction and height, where to look and extend an arm. An agreement is made together on the adaptability of the method.

Exercises and reflections

Clock face in description
1. In which situations can a clock system be used as a support for description?

Drawing according to description
2. Draw different spaces onto the surface of a table, palm and back. Discuss the different methods. What did you notice?

3. Describe and draw onto another person's back the shape of a room, directions, tables and chairs as well as the location of people present.

4. Draw a delicious meal for yourself. Describe it to another person, who will draw it on paper.

References

Collin, M-J., Kallio, M. & Tala, M. 1985. Äänikirjaopas. Näkövammaisten Kulttuuripalvelu ry. Painomarkut Oy, Helsinki.
Eeronen, R. 2002. Pistekirjoituksesta mustakirjoituksella. Kielikello 1, 34-35.
Freeman, M. 1993. In the name of the self. In a book Rewriting the self. History, memory, narrative. Routledge, England, 50-80.
Frutiger, A. 1998. Signs and symbols. Their design and meaning. Transl. Andrew Bluhm. Ebury Press, Great Britain, 43-51.
Gibson, J.J. 1962. Observations on active touch. Psychological Review Vol 69(6), 477- 491.
Gibson, J.J. 1966. The senses considered as perceptual systems. Prospect Heights, I.L.Waveland Press, Houghton Mifflin Co, Boston, USA.
Goldstein, E.B. 1989. Sensation and perception. Brooks/Cole Publishing Company, USA.
Green, S. 2000. Saavutettava museo. Liikkumis- ja toimimisesteiset kävijät opastetuilla kierroksilla. Valtion taidemuseo.
Heikkinen, A. 2008. Esteettömiä elämyksiä – miltä veistos tuntuu? Kultakuume. YLE Radio 1. 09.10.2008.
Heikkonen, M. 2005. Vihattu, rakastettu kuva. Airut 32, 1.
Hietaketo-Vieno, L., Kartovaara, M-L., Mäntylä, A., Pyötsiä, P. & Salo, A. 2000. Pisteet 2000. Pistekirjoituksen perusteet. Braille-neuvottelukunnan julkaisuja 1. Oy Edita Ab, Helsinki, 19-20, 87.
Hokkanen, R. 2009. Jumppatilanteiden kuvailua. Jyväskylän näkövammaisten koulu.
Honkanen, L. & Vartio, E. 1998. Sanoilla maalattu maisema. Tutkimus syntymäsokeiden visuaalisesta maailmankuvasta. Gummerus Kirjapaino Oy, Saarijärvi, 130-158.
Huttunen, M. 2005. Värit pintaa syvemmältä. WSOY, Porvoo.
Jakeš, J. 2003. Natural moral law and the right of deafblind people to the service of guide-interpreters. Dbl Review 32, 26-27.
Kendon, A. 1993. Human Gesture. In a book Tools, language and cognition in human evolution. Gibson, K.R. & Ingold, T. (Edit) Cambridge University Press, 48.
Kortelahti, E-L. 1979. Pitsejä virkaten ja nypläten. Risteen kirjapaino Ky, 100-101.
Lahtinen, R. 1995. Tivolissa kummitusjunan kuvailu. Kööpenhamina, Tanska.
Lahtinen, R. 2000. Haptiikasta kuvailuun. Humanistisen avoimen ammattikorkeakoulun kuvailu 1 koulutuksen (2 opintopistettä) kuvailun opetusmateriaali.
Lahtinen, R. 2001a. Ympäristön kuvailua kehoon. Tuntosarvi 1, 4-5.
Lahtinen, R. 2001b. Sharing art experiences through touch and body by drawing and kinestic movements. Museum for everyone seminar: Access to art and interpretation for people who are blind and partially sighted. Helsinki.
Lahtinen, R. 2002. Tuntoaistin ja kosketuksen käyttö aikuisten kuurosokeiden kommunikoinnissa. Kirjassa Takala, M. & Lehtomäki, E. (toim.) Kieli, kuulo ja oppiminen - kuurojen ja huonokuuloisten lasten opetus. Finn Lectura, Helsinki, 207-213.
Lahtinen, R. 2003a. Kuvailuvartti. Tuntosarvi 2, 17.
Lahtinen, R. 2003b. Päivä taktiilina. Tuntosarvi 6-7, 21–22.
Lahtinen, R. 2004. Kuvailu. Sujuva tulkkaus kuurosokeille. Selvitys kuurosokeiden tulkinkäytön kokemuksista. Julkaisuja B2, raportti 2. Suomen Kuurosokeat ry. Cityoffset Oy, Tampere, 72-91.
Lahtinen, R. 2005a. Sosiaaliset pikaviestit. Suomen Kuurosokeat ry. Julkaisuja A4. Cityoffset Oy, Tampere.
Lahtinen, R. 2005b. Kuulonäkövammaisille ja kuurosokeille kuvailu. Tuntosarvi 4, 14-15.

Lahtinen, R. 2006. Kuvailu. Kuurosokeiden tulkkipalveluopas. Kirjassa Marttila, J. (toim.) Suomen Kuurosokeat ry. Julkaisuja C4. Tehokopiointi, Tampere, 18.
Lahtinen, R. 2007. Kehosatu. Silmäterä 2, 14.
Lahtinen, R. 2008a. Haptices and haptemes. A case study of developmental process in social-haptic communication of acquired deafblind people. Doctoral dissertation. Helsinki University, Faculty of Behavioural Sciences. Cityoffset Oy, Tampere.
Lahtinen, R. 2008b. Oopperalaulaja-pantomiimin kuvailu äänellä mikrofoniin. Kuurosokeiden lomaleiri, Unkari.
Lahtinen, R., Lahtinen, M. & Paavolainen, A. 2006. Kuvailun käyttöä näkövammaisen opetuksessa. Kirjassa Takala, M. & Kontu, E. (toim.) Näkökulmia näkövammaisten opetukseen. PS-kustannus. WS Bookwell Oy, Juva, 181-191.
Lahtinen, R. & Palmer, R. 1996. Holistic Family Communication, Spoken Language by Touch is More than Just Words. 4th European Deafblind Conference Espoo, Finland.
Lahtinen, R. & Palmer, R. 1997. Theoretical Basis of Holistic Communication for Dual-Sensory Impaired People & Family Members. EUSSG & DBI Proceedings, Madrid, Spain.
Lahtinen, R. & Palmer, R. 2005. The Body Story. Creative Musical Images through Touch (CMIT). Cityoffset Oy, Tampere.
Lahtinen, R. & Pölönen, P. 2005. Kuurosokealle kuvailun mahdollisuudet. Helen Keller konferenssi, Tampere.
Lahtinen, R. & Virtanen, P. 1996. Aistien käyttäminen tulkkauksessa kuurosokean ja tulkin näkökulmasta. Uutislehti 2, NUD, Tanska.
Mactavish, J. 2001. Bravo! Miss Brown: A world without sight and sound. Cavu Inc., Canada, 41.
McLinden, M. & Graeme, D. 1999. Developing haptic perception. Eye Contact 23, 16-19.
Millar, S. 1997. Reading by touch. Routledge, UK.
Mäkinen-Vuohelainen, M. 2008. Kaikille yhteinen teatteri? Airut 22, 10-12.
Mäkinen-Vuohelainen, M. 2009. Aika ottaa askel eteenpäin, kuvailutulkkaus! Airut 2, 15-16.
Nilsson, Å. 1997. Syntolkning - konsten att måla i ord. Altt om Hjälpmedel, Nr 4.
Nimpuno, S. 1995. Kristallklart med ny proffsig syntolkning. Perspektiv 2, 15.
Nykysuomen sanakirja. 1959. WSOY, Porvoo, 683.
Othman, E. 1987. Kuunneltuja kuvia. Suomen kuvataiteen klassikoita äänikuvina. C-kas., mustavalkea painate, pistekirja ja 15 reliefikuvaa. Näkövammaisten Keskusliitto, Helsinki.
Pehrson, C.B. 2000. Kurs i syntolking lär ut vikten av engagemang. Perspektiv 9, 12-14.
Raanes, E. 2004. Kuvailu. Työteksti nro 37. (Beskrivelse, 2001). NUD, Tanska, 13.
Rakennusperintömme. 2003. Mikä on maisema? Osa 1/5, TV 1, 31.08.03.
Reyes, D. 1996. How to describe the environment to a totally deafblind person. 4th European Deafblind Conference, Espoo, Finland.
Ristimäki, T. 2008. Kuvailutekstit: kirjan kansi, tiedote, väittelijän puku, Helsingin yliopiston Siltavuorenpenger 20 D sali ja patsas. Helsingin yliopisto yleisötilaisuus 1.2.2008.
Ritala, A. 2006. Taide-elämyksiä tasa-arvoisesti. Kuvailu kuurosokealle taidenäyttelyssä eri kuvailumenetelmillä. Opinnäytetyö, Humak Helsinki, viittomakielentulkin koulutusohjelma.
Röholm, N. 2008. Äännelmä on tarina ilman sanoja. Airut 31, 12-13.
Salminen, A. 2005. Pääjalkainen. Kuva ja havainto. Koskinen, I. (toim.). Salpausselän kirjapaino, Hollola.
Sava, I. 2007. Katsomme – näemmekö? Luovuudesta, taiteesta ja visuaalisesta kulttuurista. Taideteollisen korkeakoulun julkaisusarja B81. WS Bookwell Oy, Juva, 97.
Seppänen, J. 2002. Katseen voima. Kohti visuaalista lukutaitoa. Nuorisotutkimusverkosto julkaisuja 17. Gummerus Kirjapaino Oy, Jyväskylä, 14-36.

Smith, T.B. 1994. Guidelines: Practical tips for working and socializing with deaf-blind people. Sign Media, Inc, Maryland, USA, 57-64.
Tenhami, M. 2008. Navigaattori näkövammaisen apuna. Kajastus 6, 30-31.
Tiihonen, P. 2004. Nykytaidetta ihmettelemässä. Kajastus 3, 4-6.
Turunen, T. 2005. Kuvailutulkit valmistuivat! Kajastus 6, 12-14.
Turunen, T. 2008. Työkaluja kuvailutulkille. Näkövammaisten Kulttuuripalvelu ry:n kuvailutulkkauskoulutusten pohjalta koottu opetusmateriaalipaketti. Opinnäytetyö. Humak Joutseno, Kulttuurituotannon koulutusohjelma.
Törrönen, S. & Lumiste, A. 1999. Huoneen kuvailu. Luentomoniste. Näkövammaisten kuntoutusohjaaja-koulutus, Arlainstituutti 1999-2000.
Törrönen, S. & Onnela, J. 1999. Vapaus tulla, vapaus mennä! Sokean ja heikkonäköisen liikkumistaito ja sen kehittäminen. Arlainstituutin julkaisuja 2. Gummerus Kirjapaino Oy, Saarijärvi, 47-48, 59-60.
Voipio. 2007. Piirrä selkään. Airut 9, 12.
Voutilainen, T. 2001. Kuvia Korville -projektin selostukset palvelevat näkövammaista museokävijää. Airut 29, 9.
Välttilä, P. 2008. Kuvailutulkkaus. Kultakuume, YLE Radio 1, 12.9.2008.
Waite, C. 1999. Seeing Landscapes. The creative process behind great photographs. Collins & Brown Limited, Great Britain 8, 53.
www.audiodescribe.com (1.2.2009)
www.edu.fi/oppimateriaalit/kultakausi/heletoip (20.02.2009)
www.evl.fi/liturgisetvarit (1.2.2009)
www.rnib.org.uk/audiodescription (1.2.2009)
www.vocaleyes.co.uk (1.2.2009)
Äänikirjojen lukuohjeet. 1995. Näkövammaisten kirjasto.

SUPPLEMENTARY MATERIAL

Gröhn, T. & Itkonen, S. (toim.) 2008. Kuvamatkoja maalaustaiteeseen. Opas keskusteluryhmille. Kirkkopalvelujen julkaisuja no14, 2.
Johnson, C. 1999. Valtteri ja violetti väriliitu. Gummerus Kirjapaino Oy, Jyväskylä.
Lehtinen, M. 2008. Näköstellään. Näkövammaisten kuvailmaisu. Multiprint Oy, Helsinki.
Näkemyksiä. 2005. Ensimmäiset keskisuomalaiset taiteilijat oman aikansa kuvaajina. Jyväskylän taidemuseo. www.juvaskyla.fi/taidemuseo
www.coloria.net
www.pcn.net.org (social-haptic communication, haptices and haptemes)
www.fng.fi/hugo.htm (in Swedish and English)
www.kulttuuriakaikille.fi/doc/tietopaketti_kuvailutulkkauksesta.doc (Anu Aaltonen)
www.kulttuuripalvelu.fi
www.kuurosokeat.fi/en (publication / haptices and haptemes)
www.livingpaintings.org
www.tiehallinto.fi

Publications to order:

www.earfoundation.org.uk/shop